Ed Dorn Live

POETS ON POETRY

David Lehman, General Editor
Donald Hall, Founding Editor

New titles

Elizabeth Alexander, *Power and Possibility*
John Ashbery, *Selected Prose*
Ed Dorn, *Ed Dorn Live*
Annie Finch, *The Body of Poetry*
Laura (Riding) Jackson, *The Failure of Poetry, The Promise of Language*
Alice Notley, *Coming After*
Charles Simic, *Memory Piano*
John Yau, *The Passionate Spectator*

Recently published

Dana Gioia, *Barrier of a Common Language*
Paul Hoover, *Fables of Representation*
Philip Larkin, *Further Requirements*
William Stafford, *The Answers Are Inside the Mountains*
Richard Tillinghast, *Poetry and What Is Real*

Also available, collections by

A. R. Ammons, Robert Bly, Philip Booth, Marianne Boruch,
Hayden Carruth, Amy Clampitt, Douglas Crase, Robert Creeley,
Donald Davie, Thomas M. Disch, Tess Gallagher, Linda Gregerson,
Allen Grossman, Thom Gunn, Rachel Hadas, John Haines,
Donald Hall, Joy Harjo, Robert Hayden, Edward Hirsch,
Daniel Hoffman, Jonathan Holden, John Hollander, Andrew Hudgins,
Josephine Jacobsen, Mark Jarman, Galway Kinnell, Kenneth Koch,
John Koethe, Yusef Komunyakaa, Maxine Kumin,
Martin Lammon (editor), Philip Larkin, David Lehman, Philip Levine,
Larry Levis, John Logan, William Logan, William Matthews,
William Meredith, Jane Miller, David Mura, Carol Muske,
Geoffrey O'Brien, Gregory Orr, Alicia Suskin Ostriker, Ron Padgett,
Marge Piercy, Anne Sexton, Karl Shapiro, Charles Simic,
William Stafford, Anne Stevenson, May Swenson, James Tate,
Richard Tillinghast, C. K. Williams, Alan Williamson, Charles Wright,
James Wright, and Stephen Yenser

Ed Dorn

Ed Dorn Live

LECTURES, INTERVIEWS, AND OUTTAKES

Edited by Joseph Richey

THE UNIVERSITY OF MICHIGAN PRESS
Ann Arbor

A CIP catalog record for this book is available from the British Library.

Library of Congress Cataloging-in-Publication Data

Dorn, Edward.
    Ed Dorn live : lectures, interviews, and outtakes / edited by
Joseph Richey.
        p.   cm. — (Poets on poetry)
    Includes bibliographical references.
    ISBN-13: 978-0-472-09862-0 (cloth : acid-free paper)
    ISBN-10: 0-472-09862-4 (cloth : acid-free paper)
    ISBN-13: 978-0-472-06862-3 (pbk. : acid-free paper)
    ISBN-10: 0-472-06862-8 (pbk. : acid-free paper)
    I. Richey, Joseph.   II. Title.

PS3507.O73277E32   2007
813'.54—dc22   2007010655

Contents

Preface

By Joseph Richey

Edward Merton Dorn was proud to be from the most fertile soil scraped off the receding Wisconsin glacier, in the southern Illinois town of Villa Grove on April 2, 1929. Poet Robert Duncan introduced Ed Dorn as one "born under a dark star," six months before the stock market crash and the start of the Great Depression. His father vanished down the eastbound railroad tracks before Ed's birth. They never met. His early education was limited to a one-room schoolhouse. But it expanded enormously under the influence of a handful of teachers and over the course of his fifty-plus years of scholarship.

Dorn went west initially for fun and work as a lumberjack and day laborer, later on assignment from his teacher Charles Olson at Black Mountain College, in 1950–51 and 1953. See *A Bibliography on America for Ed Dorn.* The assignment lasted decades, resulting in *The Shoshoneans, Recollections of Gran Apacheria, Gunslinger, Westward Haut, Way West,* and many articles and reviews in the magazine *Rolling Stock.*

Dorn wrote over forty books, but he earned his modest income and short-lived retirement from thirty-three years of teaching: at the University of Colorado (twenty-two years), the University of Kansas, the University of California at San Diego, the University of California at Riverside, Northeastern Illinois University, Kent State University, the University of Essex (in England), and Idaho State University, and from speaking venues and poetry readings all over America and England.

This book was compiled from the best available recordings and transcripts gathered in the years directly preceding Dorn's death in 1999. It provides a sense of Ed Dorn the professor and poet, and gives him the floor to vent, to blow his horn, and to explain his poetics.

Dorn treated the difficult labor of writing as a serious business, but one well mixed with pleasure. His students have vivid memories of Ed Dorn live, in action, in autodidactic splendor. In this book, I hope that they find the words of poet Edward Merton Dorn alive and well, and that newcomers get a glimpse of first-person Ed and his system of poetics.

Philip Whalen called a poem "a picture or graph of a mind moving." Although the lectures and interviews in this volume constitute such a record, Dorn insisted that his spoken word be distinguished from the written. He warned of readers' tendency to confuse interviews and lectures with actual writing. Stylistic differences aside, he knew that some statements are easily misconstrued when their context is ignored, context that would be supplied deliberately in a written text. He provided oversight in the editing of these transcriptions but did not apply his writing hand to them. Several interviews and lectures, "Waying the West," "The Last Interviews," and "Poetry Is a Difficult Labor" were edited significantly and cannot be considered complete or verbatim.

Two previous books compile interviews and opinions of Edward Dorn: *Interviews* (1980), and *Views* (1980), both edited by Donald Allen. *Ed Dorn Live* collects material generated after these compilations, as well as lectures and interviews unavailable to them.

This book was created in gratitude to Ed Dorn, from friends, readers, and students, with all due obeisance and fealty.

Grateful acknowledgment is made to Kush at Cloud House Poetry Archives; Steve Dickison at the American Poetry Archive at San Francisco State University; the Naropa Audio Archive at Naropa University's Allen Ginsberg Library, Boulder, Colorado; Brad Westbrook at Mandeville Special Collections Library's New Poetry Archive at the University of California at San Diego; the Pacifica Radio Archive, David Barsamian at Alternative Radio, and David Franks for making his personal audio archive available.

I thank Dorn's colleagues at the Department of English at the University of Colorado—especially Peter Michelson, Paul

Levitt, Lee Krauth, John Stevenson, and Patricia Limerick at the Center for the American West—for giving the job its first big push; and interviewers Paul Dresman, Matthew Cooperman, Effie Mihopoulos, Tom Pickard, Tandy Sturgeon, Kevin Bezner, Dale Smith, Michael Price, and Iain Sinclair for the generous provision of their material.

Grateful acknowledgment is also made to Randy Roark, Rudy Mesicek, and Virginia Perry for a few transcriptions, and Anne Becher, Randall Schroth, and Meg Knox for keen reading and comments that were helpful.

Special thanks are in order to Jennifer Dunbar Dorn, who helped advance the work at every turn. And last I thank Edward Dorn himself, who did not tolerate my naïveté, and as a result, did not merely complement my education, but provided a direction for lifelong learning.

Introduction

By Peter Michelson

The postmodern division of the house of American poetry, about 1950, identified two broad inclinations of younger poets. One line preferred a traditional formality of verse style and produced a conversational, poised, rhetorically dense verse that one might expect to find in the *New Yorker* or *Atlantic*. Such poets as James Dickey, Donald Hall, Robert Lowell, and Sylvia Plath worked that line. The other sort was more flamboyant, raucous, and experimental and was characterized by the Beat and Black Mountain poetics of Allen Ginsberg and Charles Olson. Olson's premise of "projective verse" became the theoretical guidon for what came to be called the Black Mountain school of poetry. Its name came from Black Mountain College, of which Olson was rector. Edward Dorn attended Black Mountain in 1950 and 1951 to study poetics, returning in 1953 to study with Charles Olson.

While variations on projective verse were widely practiced and debated through the postmodern era, Dorn became one of its most prominent practitioners. The serial publication of *Gunslinger* in the late 1960s and through the 1970s established Dorn as one of the most vital poets on the American literary scene. A plausible model for a distinctly western American poetics is the poetic legacy of Ed Dorn and his Slinger.

The poem *Gunslinger,* a brilliantly brittle mock epic romp ostensibly through the western American landscape, is a lacerating satire of cultural arrogance, industrialism, and the national ethos. It addressed the question, first invoked by Walt Whitman and subsequently by William Carlos Williams, about the nature of an American idiom. Dorn created a simulated idiom that was both western and American, synthesized from literary, cinematic, street, and historical models. From these sources, Dorn's idiom evoked American mythology, history, sociology, and political economy to create a satire at once classical, American, and western.

Dorn's *Gunslinger* is to poets what Jack Palance's performance in *Shane* is to actors. For both, its incisive menace is mediated by a distinctively graceful intellection. This quality permeates *Gunslinger* and the later poems. It is also the quality that makes Dorn's caustic attentions to the culture so much more engaging than the predictable ironies of the culture itself. Dorn is a writer's poet, wafting a special aroma of attention, of information, of intelligence, and of speech into the collective imaginative atmosphere. He is also an experimental poet, one whose experiments are not simply their own excuse for being, but have a clear sense of focus and function. He is the paradigm of what is meant by the cutting edge when it is understood that the edge is cutting through one thing to get to another, and this is the only way to get there.

As he notes in these interviews, that dramatic period of history between 1968 and 1975 is when he developed his documentary aesthetic, "to seriously use—instead of . . . my own personal objections to the behavior of this so-called society—to actually use events as part of the play." *Play* here means not only the unfolding drama of events but also Dorn's witty, irreverent, and moral transformation of crude ironies into aesthetic perception. It reconstitutes Ezra Pound's epic model in the sense of a poem containing history.

Again in these interviews, Dorn offers his addendum to Robert Creeley's famous epithet, "Since form is 100% of what you see and a direct application of what the poet feels, form is in everything an announcement and expression of reality: Form is always an extension of everything."

Accordingly, each of his books *Gunslinger, Recollections of Gran Apachería, Abhorrences, Languedoc Variorum* is a distinctive experiment with a different form. And *Languedoc Variorum,* still in progress at his death, was perhaps the most precocious departure from poetic conventions in postmodern American poetry, with its incorporation of staid scholarly apparatus with bottom-of-the-screen Nasdaq stock reports and a vigorous narrative apologia for the heretical dovetailed with a documentary critique of the Crusades and Crusaders.

Poetry's responsibility, in Dorn's poetics, is cultural, historical, and intellectual. Experiment is properly used to those ends. Concrete poetry, sound poetry, language poetry have a certain amusement quotient. But, says Dorn, "Experimental in our time has largely come to mean incomprehensible, and I certainly don't have any truck with that. . . . I think that the poem should be pitched at as intellectual a level as you're capable of. . . . That's what exploration and experimentation *are* to me . . . the only kind that I would have any respect for." In fact, Dorn has a profound respect for literary tradition, as manifest in the conclusion to his statement to the Charles Olson conference in 1978, "Part of the reason I'm interested in the 18th century almost exclusively is because it's an outrageous present position to take, [and] in the literary sense, I find it a great taste to my mind. I also endlessly promote the prose of Johnson in, say, *The Lives of the Poets* as being my sense of how to correct the drift." That there is a drift to correct and that it might best be done via an "outrageous present position" suggests Dorn's testy relation to the American polity. In his 1992 interview in the *American Poetry Review*, with his writing of *Abhorrences* through the 1980s he consciously cultivated a poetics with attitude. "One of the basic propositions of [*Abhorrences*] is that the only poetry that really matters is the poetry that exhibits a certain kind of aggression toward the readers. I don't see any reason to write any other kind of poetry at this moment . . . given where we're at nobody is going to be aesthetically enlightening." In a 1984 interview at the University of Wisconsin, he identified the philosophical basis of his critique of where we're at, in the context of political poetry and First World poets appropriating Third World griefs as their own: "The point for me here is the simple fact that sensibility is no substitute for consciousness. . . . politics in poetry really amounts to enunciation."

Whether in terms of history or current events Dorn's posture was often outrageous and aggressive, which is to say heretical to popular sentiments and received wisdom. If offensiveness is your principal implement of assault, the more offense the better. But in Dorn's work offensiveness is not an indulgence. It is an aesthetic strategy calculated "to bestir the prun'ed tongues" of the quiescent vox populi. In 1999 he says, "Heretics are the only responsible citizens and heresy the only responsible position." He goes on to say, "I don't consider myself a heretic in any important sense." If Edward Dorn was not himself a heretic, he quite distinctly fashioned a brilliantly incisive poetic voice in the eloquent tradition of Jeremiah, Aristophanes, Juvenal, Dante, Pope, Swift, Zola, Pound, Lawrence, and, after all, Rexroth and Olson.

Dorn himself approved the occasion of this collection of interviews and lectures. He was active in the editing and compilation with editor Joe Richey until the cancer he had been fighting off for nearly three years finally wore him out. One reason Joe Richey took on the monumental task here, and was encouraged to do so by friends and colleagues, is that Ed Dorn, like the Dr. Johnson he so admired, is so eminently quotable. However briefly you might be in his presence, you recognized a vitality of intelligence and being stunningly incisive in articulation. His language, whether in verse or conversation, had what the Greeks called *aretē*. It stopped you in your tracks. What seems exclusively extemporaneous turns out to be not merely witty but substantive and considered. Ed's surfaces are quick and sharp, but they are also cut deep. Quite apart from whether you agree with him, you are always aware of a language that reflects distinctive imagination engaging the world. Where he sees evil—and he does, damn anachronism, speak unapologetically of good and evil in the world—he nails it as deftly and definitively as ever Martin Luther did his theses to the door. Ronald Reagan, Dorn said in 1991, was one of the "greatest hirelings of the dark powers the world has ever known." Even as incisive articulation was crucial to his arsenal, so was hyperbole. The result, whether in conversation, verse, or prose, was a bold language of large claims, arresting perceptions, extraordinary and relentless intelligence, and laser beam wit.

This book collects the commentary of his later years and last days. It is a mature punctuation to previous collections. It is especially important for its synthesizing of Dorn's views on poetic experimentation, the distinction between consciousness and sensibility, and heretical intellection, which is to say the components of his poetics of aggression. Dorn wrote very little critical prose. Accordingly, his caustic, improvisational voice now constitutes the record of his critical thought. And, given the acerbic, improvisational character of his personal and literary styles, this is very likely the most fitting vehicle for the transport of his legacy.

On the Authority of Root Meanings, the External, and the Making of *Gunslinger,* circa 1967

At the request of poets Allen Ginsberg and Anne Waldman,
Ed Dorn gave a series of lectures and a reading of his poems at
the newly founded Naropa Institute and its Jack Kerouac School
of Disembodied Poetics in June 1977. It was the first of many
lectures he would give in Boulder, Colorado. The invitation to
Naropa's summer program in 1977 would land Dorn a teach-
ing post at the University of Colorado, from which he would
retire twenty-one years later. Even though Dorn operated without
a college degree, having never accepted a diploma from Black
Mountain College, CU's Department of English hired Dorn on
the merits of his published books and his literary and historical
ties to Charles Olson. His unorthodox style suited the depart-
ment's young Creative Writing Program.

Dorn's lectures were fast and loose from the get-go. As prepa-
ration for this lecture, Dorn had assigned Edward Abbey's essay
"The Great American Desert" and J. B. Jackson's "The Public
Landscape." But he begins with a warning about relying on any
one dictionary, and ultimately implores the young writers to
authorize meaning themselves. Dorn discusses the notions of "the
assignment" and "the external," and whether his poem
"Gunslinger" is an example of either one, or both.

June 13, 1977

Knowing the root meaning of a word of course doesn't necessarily force its proper use. And in fact it rarely does. Words have
habits embedded in them very deeply. To get at a root meaning
one needs ten or twenty dictionaries of a very special nature. It's
no good just going to Webster or even the biggest Skeats.

Mr. Walter William Skeat compiled the big etymological dictionary. But that too simply provides a summary of where the root is. You certainly don't get the network or the grid of what it is. You get a summary of someone else's exploration of what it is. That would be one "authority." Skeat is one "authority." It's not necessarily the root, but it's one "authority." This same phenomenon operates all over the place, in almost everything: the acceptance of truth as authority. Authority simply being the summation of somebody's opinion of what authority is.

You have to operate around a word according to its present problems. For example, in J. B. Jackson's essay "The Public Landscape," he needs to introduce how the "public" or "political" landscape is quite distinct from the "natural landscape," or the "economic landscape," or the "private landscape," though no more important than these.

"Few of us realize that there is another kind of megastructure, a megastructure in terms of a whole environment; one of the oldest creations of man. This megastructure consisting of the environment organized by man can be called the public landscape. A more correct term would be the political landscape; but since we associate that word not with citizenship as we should, but with politicians and politics, the term public is more effective."

This essay is found in J. B. Jackson's *Landscapes,* edited by Ervin H. Zube. Zube is from the Department of Landscape Architecture at the University of Massachusetts, and perhaps was a student of Jackson's. I don't know that much about Jackson but I'll tell you what I know. He was the editor of a magazine called *Landscape* in Santa Fe, New Mexico, in the fifties and the early sixties. The magazine perhaps still goes on under another editor. He graduated from Harvard. He's got what sounds to me like a very New England kind of name—John Brinckerhoff Jackson. He presently lectures at Harvard and Berkeley—kind of half the year, on the subject of landscape. Back in his Santa Fe days, he wore a leather jacket and rode a motorcycle. He still does, I think. He's quite an elegant and very engaging lecturer. And the lecture I heard in Berkeley this past winter was on truck culture, in which he set out some of the ideas that I have already gone into, I think. Have you got the notes on that?

Student: Yeah, about driving in the . . .

Dorn: Yeah, right.

This will lead us further to the heart of the city—according to this definition: that automobiles are middle class; and trucks are democratic and classless precisely because they redistributed the economy at a time when in order to be a shopkeeper, just prior to the truck, you had to have the capitalization to afford a carload of something on the railroad, and to capitalize yourself was a much greater strain. But with the truck came the mom-and-pop store and mom-and-pop industry in which small amounts of things could be ordered—like ten loaves of bread, a hundred pounds of wheat or whatever, a few nails. And it would be delivered to your store. You wouldn't have to have a strong team and wagon to go down and fetch it from the depot. And this then started the spread of warehouses and the warehouse mentality almost immediately. And since that needs space, it all gravitates to the edge of things. Air trucks and things like that immediately suggest themselves. In fact, it already looks like this is the last grand moment of the highway, in every respect. And it's not because the Arabs are "cutting off our oil," but because the whole thing has become too tedious. Since we live in a culture which is quite particular about the tedium it will undergo, I see highways as on the way out.

In the Jackson passage I see actually the same surroundings that one has in a poem in which the linguistic surroundings can prompt redefinition on the spur of the moment, according to one's feel for the galaxies of words. They point *forward* very often, these kinds of definitions within the poem. Certain words *signal* the deepest sense a word possesses, because its meaning is created in its environment and, in that sense, is way beyond, and more vital to the word than, the dictionary.

This is not in any sense to lower the value of the dictionary. It's certainly the heart of the culture, really—The Dictionary . . . it's *the* book. But the dictionary then changes slowly over the years to accommodate what's been happening to the language. And it should be slow to accommodate because, of course, language is so massively trivial most of the time that whatever time the dictionary takes to get to it is certainly no more than it should have. In fact, the shakiest dictionaries are the quickest to react. It's a bit like translating the Bible to accommodate the lessening literacy of those people who think they need to have a

Bible. There are dictionaries like that also. The Random House Dictionary is an example of that. It's entertaining.

Writing, in general of course, is the chord emanating from the source which measures the length of how far the word has strayed from its origin. So in that sense there is no such thing as the misuse of a word. That's actually an organic impossibility. The only thing that happens is the length of this chord, which is not the same thing as a mistake.

Dorn: You have read Ed Abbey on "The Great American Desert" and J. B. Jackson's articles. So the assignment is to write a poem from the completely external. To write a poem from the completely external of not less than a 100 words and not more than 150.

Student: Okay, quick consultation with one of my colleagues here. What do you mean by "external"?

Dorn: I was hoping nobody would ask that question.

[Students grumbling.]

Dorn: Yeah. Well, all right. Just a sec.
    Well, what do you think? What do you think that means?

Student: Not an autobiographical observation, but it's external to itself.

Dorn: Yeah, that would be okay. That would, I mean, be a very small percentage of what it ought to mean. But it wouldn't be wrong.

Student: Well, what's the answer?

Dorn: I was told that I only had to make an assignment. I wasn't told that I had to do it.

Student: Can't you explain that?

Dorn: Yeah. I just thought it would be so obvious because of that word "external"—that it would be like a question that would be there but un-askable.
    Ah, let's see. The thing of it is: if I try to hit it and I get it wrong, you'll be misled.

Student: Is it anything like . . . .

Dorn: It's not a riddle.

Student: Well, is it something like that William Carlos Williams's line "not in ideas but in things."

Dorn: Okay, you've forced me to do it.

No. It's not like that.

That process is the great dictum for giving the emotions traction, I'd say. You can see the value of the attempt to so focus the mind that you don't get all this lyrical shimmy you get from philosophy and so forth. And thus it's quite useful.

But that's not what I mean at all. And in fact that's quite an old and traditional idea in our system now. That would be, since we've moved through so many ages, we already have, say, nineteenth-century elements in our own past which you could say would be like 1938 could be our, you know, perverse Victorian. This sounds nineteenth century, twentieth century–nineteenth century. And that's like: Williams is our Wordsworth.

[Pause.]

One thing I've really learned here at Naropa is the value of the Buddhist pause. It's worth a lot, let me tell you, because I always heretofore thought that I had to talk *all the time,* and it would be a strain.

In other words, I'm talking about the opposite. I'm talking about the lattice of reality operating on you completely. In other words, you're to have as little to do with the poem as possible. I should think, since I defined the assignment, I'd say that would be the standard of success.

"Don't take it personally" would be another way to put it.

I guess the poem has traded its dullness and its authority and it believability for a lot of other things, like jiveyness and beauty and persuasiveness and oratorical-ness. It's traded a lot for rhapsody. Rhapsody? Yeah, I think that one measure of success of the modern poem is that it, to a certain extent, is *rhapped.*

Certainly the Jackson article has got something to do with what I mean. A kind of relaxation of the grammatical language I'd like to see in an external poem. I mean that assignment would ask you to give up the struggles of the "questions of poetry," whatever they may be for you. This kind of assignment requires some judgment because (unlike another method in which the lyric sensibility is sort of skimming the aesthetic possibilities of what's *in there,* or to a certain extent *out there*) with the lyric, it's really not that far out. The projection is far out, but where it's coming from obviously can't be. The lyric is somewhat like what astronomers say of the periphery of a black hole; that's the Schwarzschild radius. The Schwarzschild radius is a mathematical formula to demarcate that point where everything goes in for good, and outside it, it doesn't.

This other sense, which doesn't have even a label (like "external"), is streaming in.

If I keep talking I'm going to reveal it as an extremely simple idea when, in the first place, it had a certain, nice complication to it.

See, this is the danger of over-explanation. I think now I've already truncated your possibilities with it to a certain extent. You see? It's best left alone.

Well, that's the assignment. So we can leave that, right?

Just remember that everything that's gone on so far in some way is actually the explanation of the assignment.

June 20, 1977

We were talking about "the assignment." We all know that in poetry in a quite orthodox sense, there aren't any assignments. There really aren't any "assignments" in poetry. By definition, there can't be an assignment for poetry. One can elaborate various conditions for oneself and they can take the place of it, but they're never assignments. They're not even assignments if you say, "I'm going to assign myself a poem." It's still not an assignment. It's still self-generative in that sense. Assignments almost always come from someone else. In that sense I could, if it were possible to give you an assignment for poetry, I could do that because I'm, you know, I'm able to assign. Or you could assign me. But that's just getting extremely over-elaborate and complicated with a definition that's essentially quite simple.

Assignments are for study, actually, or for research, even when it comes to the writing of anything. Writing is such an ambulatory mechanism in the mental sense. Some people get quite physical when they write and stand up and bang the typewriter or walk around and shout and so forth. It is actually quite a physical process really, much more than people imagine who imagine that it's rather mental.

I was talking about assignment and wondering if I had assigned myself *Slinger*. I still don't think so.

One could call it a verse-work in four parts with a bridge; that bridge is "The Cycle." It's written in sections called "books," not quite so arbitrarily to get away from letters or cantos or all the other earlier twentieth-century habits, but because they felt connected, in themselves, conclusive stories in a way. More like a book than a canto, which is a movement of a large thing. I suppose it's a more prosaic reference. When we hear "book"— that's opposed to canto, and it dissociates itself with that definition from song as such.

Where have I been hearing, "The world is a bridge, don't build on it"? I've not been hearing that around? Where have I heard that? Or did I read that? Did they say that? What I was thinking was this: the section of this long verse-work called "The Cycle" spans like a bridge and, in a way, there's nothing on it.

Gunslinger starts out with a fair amount of velocity, and not much hope. It's rather tight in the sense that there's a certain anxiety to do something I hadn't done before, and for which there wasn't that much precedence immediately available to look at. So, it's faster than it is quick. And it's probing. The speech is a little stiff. It's rather arch. Looking back, it seems to compensate for the fact that the way is being groped. There is the arch of its formality in the beginning, which is a rhetorical formality, not necessarily a poetic formality.

> I met in Mesilla
> The Cautious Gunslinger
> of impeccable personal smoothness
> and slender leather encased hands
> folded casually
> to make his knock.
> He would show you his map.

Why did I set my thing in Mesilla? It was always a kind of a provocative town for me because Billy the Kid hung around there a lot, and it was an important crossroads, it was the territorial capital of New Mexico briefly before Santa Fe I think. I had a lot of interpenetration of that kind of romantic Spanish civilization of the Southwest and the Anglo-Saxon zeal to be aware of it.

> There is your domain.
> Is it the domicile it looks to be
> or simply a retinal block
> of seats in,
> he will flip the phrase
> the theater of impatience

It attempts to be subjunctive and provocative in that sense: a question that is not actually a question. It's as arbitrary as Dadaism in Switzerland. "Is it the domicile it *looks to be*," you see, none of this is meant to be real. It "looks to be." That's the signal that distance is being enforced already.

"The theater of impatience" is a guerilla-ism, softened and molded and made neutral in a way in order to free the dramatic impetus.

I'm speaking in retrospect so this is not a calculation at all because, at the time, as is often the case, when you can sense you're ready for something you hope is big, you best not question what might get to look strange in the writing, or not look like your habit or something. It's best to let it rip. And even maybe through a certain interest in it, as you're doing it, enhance its weirdness in that way.

So it gets rhetorically strange right off, then, throughout the course of the work, it gets rhetorically relaxed as the mechanism becomes understood and there is a certain confidence gained that it will run. The attention then can be switched to other matters—relaxed that way. In other words, there comes a point after a certain time where some things will take care of themselves. And I don't mean that the writing is automatic (whatever that means), "automatic writing." I don't mean automatic writing but that the writing is automatic. I don't mean either of those two things, but that it becomes self-sufficient in a certain way.

Well, as I've noted, I went over it later and took out certain references that were so local to my own position at the time that I thought they would tend to destroy the whole fabric which was not supposed to be so located. There were certain things of course that were not possible to excise for reasons I never understood aside from instinct.

I'm really just trying to lay out where *Gunslinger* is coming from in 1967, a year of some notoriety. I would really like to lead your minds into the past that the poem occupies without suggesting that it's dependent on that past, or that you are either, or that there's any relationship with it really.

> If it is where you are,
> the footstep in the flat above
> in a foreign land

I sought to get rid of this line, and actually would still like to, but couldn't and can't.

> or any shimmer the city
> sends you
> the prompt sounds
> of a metropolitan nearness
> he will unroll the map of locations.

Again, an instance of risking a certain brittleness to get rid of a topical and current softness; for instance, "he will unroll the map of love" would have been true to its time; and, in fact, was. That's rewriting. Are you following now what I'm saying?

> His knock resounds
> inside its own smile, where?
> I ask him is my heart.

> Not this pump he answers
> already artificial and bound
> touching me
> with his leather finger
> as the Queen of hearts burns
> from his gauntlet into my eyes.

The introduction of the Gunslinger is my heart. That was my first solution of how to make something talk inside a poem without quotation marks, without the conventions of theatrical transcription, without anything except punctuation. So we have "where?," which is the end of the line, back to where you can formulate a system for ending the line. The present tense relieves this problem that I've been speaking of. Here's an instance of the line's own necessity. It's the only possible way to ask a question and get an answer without interrupting the poetics in the deadly way that poetics are interrupted when quotations are in a poem. I don't mean just quotation marks, but any overt move to activate voices other than those voices that are understood to be the voices motivated by, or under the control of, the Muse, which are ghost voices in a way.

> Flageolets of fire
> he says there will be.
> This is for your sadly missing heart
> the girl you left
> in Juarez, the blank
> political days press her now
> in the narrow adobe
> confines of the river town
> her dress is torn
> by the misadventure of
>   her gothic research
>
> The mission bells are ringing
> in Kansas.

A kind of an ad lib list actually. It never meant anything to me, and still doesn't. It's just possibilities of where one might have been, or anybody might have been. Here the problem is still imagining one's self in conversation with something hopefully not one's self.

"The mission bells are ringing in Kansas" is a reference to what is an assignment, which is content. Content actually can be an assignment quite easily. One can be assigned to learn. I was assigned the West when I was a student. So this is almost an inside reference. It could easily be a footnote. "The mission bells are ringing / in Kansas" meant to summarize for me everything I know or everything I know as a student of that condition, and everything you might know either as a student or, if not as a student, as a auditor of your culture about the Kansas railheads, the Spanish flirtation, *para donde va Coronado,* wheat, the Swedenborgian communities, Kansas mysticism, whatever.

> Have you left something out:
> Negative, says my Gunslinger,
> no *thing* is omitted.

That's just straight CB and out. And that's italicized in order to be a very large mystificatory barrier—"no *thing* is omitted."

When this edition was collected, I put in these following lines to flesh that a little bit. They are new, and not in the earlier books.

> Time is more fundamental than space.
> It is, indeed, the most persuasive
> of all categories
> in other words
> there's plenty of it.
> And it stretches things themselves
> until they blend into one,
> so if you've seen one thing
> you've seen them all.

I was reading John Randolph Lucas studies in different concepts of time. That's actually a line stolen pure from his first page. The rest is my own commentary. It is meant to give a sort of playful pomposity—a little kick at this point which it didn't have before, and, at the same time to set up, then, man's habits, which are to make a statement like that, and then try to cut it out; "in other words / there's plenty of it." It's equally important to formulate it and to unformulate it, or vernacularize it again, in other words, again in reference to what I've said earlier, to try to include greater precision of the vernacular. The quicker, harder, more inexorable precision of the vernacular, which at the same time seems very, very loose and offhand. That's where its power comes from, because there are no themes, really. There's no story, there are no themes, and there's no point in the whole thing. In fact, if it has a salvation, that's it.

Student: Do you tip your hat to T. S. Eliot, with the importance of time in *Four Quartets*? Or just try to put it in that kind of tradition?

Dorn: My feeling about influence is that all influences are there. The question of whether they're conscious influences is another matter, and I don't feel they are. I feel . . . There's a certain way in which I can't define the influence of Williams in the management and maintenance of the line, let's say. Although I wouldn't be able to say precisely how, but I would admit that influence must be large, more actually than Olson, who I discovered had a much too turgid and complicated a line to be of use for this kind of work. This kind of statement, no matter how uneasy and difficult the content may get, calls for a fairly simple procedure. So the length of this line, as you can see, varies, from not quite short to very little beyond medium, pretty much throughout. The "Cycle" departs from that, but that's another question, which I'll take up later.

> I held the reins of his horse
> while he went into the desert
> to pee. Yes, he reflected
> when he returned, that's less.
>
> How long, he asked
> have you been in this territory.

"Pee" and "territory" are meant to be a hard, distant rhyme, which happens a lot in this work. And another problem I had with rhyme was that I knew after a certain time that I was going to let this go on for quite a while; therefore, I had to steer clear of any regularities that might get to be seen as overpowering regularities. Yet the echo of rhyme or the quick juxtaposition of hard rhyme, in certain rhythmic patterns, obviously can really tamp your verse a lot. It can be a tightening mechanism too, for lines you don't want to get tight in other ways. So obviously I didn't want to throw out that as a means. So this is already trying a very delayed, asymmetrical and off rhyme. I was interested in making as much initial complication in that sense as possible, while still keeping it very thin, and on the surface.

> Years I said. Years
> Then you will know where we can have
> a cold drink before sunset and then a bed
> will be my desire
> if you can find one for me
> I have no wish to continue

my debate with men,
my mare lathers with tedium
her hooves are dry
Look they are covered with the alkali
of the enormous space
between here and formerly.
Need I repeat, we have come
without sleep from Nuevo Laredo.

And why do you have such a horse
Gunslinger? I asked. Don't move
he replied
the sun rests deliberately
on the rim of the sierra.

The horizon is very important; those kind of loci are really the story, the story of the attention. And it's actually just talk between somebody who's in a place talking to somebody who's passing through. The experience is a common human one, in which the person stuck gets interested in the person passing through, and eventually the stuck person goes with the person passing through. It's an old American habit. Very often the only excuse we need to leave is to run into somebody who's leaving. It's a fundamental American transient trait. It may be more common at some times than it is at others, and by analyzing that habit you can actually tell a lot about the state of society at that point.

Then, the big external reference.

And where will you now I asked.
Five days northeast of here
depending of course on whether one's horse
is of iron or flesh
there is a city called Boston
and in that city there is ahotel
whose second floor has been let
to an inscrutable Texan named Hughes

The way that line is disposed is meant to signal that we're not going to have any truck with predictable rhetoric in that way. It means to signal that both those possibilities still reside in English, for English speakers anywhere, even though they may have dropped the business of "an history" for "a history" or "an hotel" or "a hotel." So here it's made one word, "ahotel," to actually correct a certain American sloppiness over that question, a certain American reluctance to do either one or the other. So that's just simply there as a very calculated piece of instruction—"ahotel." In fact, the proper way of saying it is to just make it that word—not "hotel," but to give it the indefinite article as part of it's own body.

> Howard? I asked
> The very same.
> And what do you mean by inscrutable,
>   oh Gunslinger?
> I mean to say that He
> has not been seen since 1833.
>
> But when have you found him my Gunslinger
> what will you do, oh what will you do?
> You would not know
> that the souls of old texans
> are in jeopardy in a way not common
> to other men, my singular friend.
>
> You would not know
> of the long plains night
> where they carry on
> and arrange their genetic duels
> with men of other states—
> so there is a longhorn bull half mad
> half deity
> who awaits an account from me
> back of the sun you nearly disturbed
> just then.
> Lets have that drink.
>
> . . .
>
> Shit, Slinger! you still got that
> marvelous creature, and who is this
> funny talker, you pick him up
> in some sludgy seat of higher
> learnin, Creeps! you always did
> hang out with some curious refugees.
> Anyway come up and see me
> and bring your friend, anytime
> if you're gonna be in town we

> got an awful lot to talk about
> for instance, remember that man
> you was always looking for
> name of Hughes?
> Howard? I asked
> You got it—that was
> the gent's first handle
> a texas dynamiter he was
> back in '32
> always turned my girls on a lot
> when he blew In,
> A man in the house
> is worth 2 in the street.

That's a Mae West line, this is really just the vocabulary of being stoned in the sixties. It's absolutely right across 1967. The reportages are meant to be in tune with that time. All the books are. They keep track of the segments of the time they're in. This first book does perhaps more so.

> Then there was an interlude
> in which the brawl before our
> indented eyes went on.
>
> Auto-destruction he breathed
> and I in that time was
> suspended
> as if in some margin of the sea
> I saw the wading flanks
> of horses spread in energy.

Meaning to rhyme with "of the sea."

I wish now I hadn't come on quite so smart, although it's all right. But it introduces what is to be the character. And again I think one can sense that it's already a character and not the pronoun. This is the first overt use of "I," and then the horse gets introduced.

As this got down the road (and this is not very far down the road but it's already off), it's pretty evident that I started out with a mere character and a half. The supply was that low. So when I saw the possibility of "I" become a focal point, I said, it still only makes two characters in a way, and I had no real idea of where they were going to come from. So they were kind of summoned one at a time, or beckoned in some sense, as the necessity for them arose. And I think this is actually a good example of how the writing of these books came about. It wasn't efficient, but it was fairly straightforward and quick once it got under way.

The preparation was elaborate, not in a charted sense, but the amassing of phrases and the tying four or five lines here and there to see what might happen, maybe the inking in whole sections, would go on long before I would attempt to put it together. When then I thought the material was of a sufficient quantity to float what I was calling a book, then I would get it all out and reduce it (because it'd be just everywhere, so I would sort of try to get it on pieces of paper, so that I could actually look at it).

This might go on for months, and all the time I was reading, of course. I read a lot for this; not as a means of research, but I tended to read things that I knew would be provocative to it in various ways. Actually it's pretty evident what I was reading [Heidegger, Strauss, Lucas, press of the 1960s news media]. Writing some sections, I would feel they were so stable that I could actually use them as bases for various emotions in it. Largely I would just write it and maybe spend a couple of weeks rewriting it.

Remember I was educated at a time, which was probably the last time in this country, when a systematic education in the humanities was still an ideal. Not that I got one, but it was an ideal. So that my tendency has been to at least seem orderly. I mean, insofar as I can. The limitations are pretty strict because that's set for you by the time you're sixteen or seventeen at the latest. If you haven't got a system by then you're never going to get it.

What Black Mountain did was to teach that a system was ideal—intellectually ideal, but improbable. So you were supposed to do the best you could. It results in one's being enamored of learning in the end, which is fine. I'd as soon love learning as anything else.

On the Making of *Gunslinger,* circa Chicago, 1971

As "Gunslinger" grew in recognition, Dorn grew more elusive about the anti-epic. Only in occasional lectures did he discuss the work. While he was teaching at the University of Colorado in October 1991, Professor Peter Michelson asked Dorn to visit his graduate English class in Recent Poetry to answer a few questions about the work. Remembering Ed Dorn's subterfuges and divergent mind, Michelson yields to Dorn's desire to talk about Chicago in 1971, tycoon styles of Howard Hughes, Michael Milken, and Ross Perot, and the CIA Drug Connection, "Gunslinger" and "The Aeneid."

Peter Michelson: In the preface to the *Collected Poems,* you say, "From near the beginning I have known my work to be theoretical in nature and poetic by virtue of its inherent tone."

Now that seems to me to apply as well to *Gunslinger.* First of all, am I right? And, assuming that I am, would you talk about that statement—the theoretical and the tone making it poetic?

Ed Dorn: Well, that's one of those kind of statements in which one obviously tries to cover as much ground as possible, hoping that nothing will be noticed.

But I suppose it actually applies more to *Gunslinger* than it does to most of the poems in the *Collected Poems.* If you're writing with kind of a big sweep, whether that sweep is sardonic, serious, proto-, pseudo-, whatever, it doesn't make any difference. It's still the sweep, because once you depart from "just things," it becomes theory automatically. "No ideas but in things" I always thought was one of the most awful statements ever made in America, and I put my face against that instantly. It was an intent to shackle the spirit to the ground just like—nail it to its own tattoo. I thought, "Well, that's cool for a country doctor in a suburban New Jersey town, but it's certainly not going to be good enough for me." After all, Dr. Williams received his education at the University of Pennsylvania, where he learned how to cut out your liver and did a pretty good job of it.

But poetry for me has been my education, and it still is. So, I still work out of the reference books and as well as my own sensibility or street sensibility. In other words, I never left school. If you spent virtually your entire life in school, your view of the world and your view of time is really distorted—it's very perverted and distorted. You don't have the same sense that other folks do your age.

Michelson: What about that inherent tone that makes it theoretical?

Dorn: Well, if it sounds like it's poetry, it is poetry. That's about the only thing we've got left. You know, there's an awful lot of stuff that parades as poetry but is not poetry and mainly because it doesn't sound like poetry. People make an awful lot of really difficult cases to explain what's simply a fact of life: you know it's poetry or you know it's not poetry. It's not actually defined in terms of what used to be; e.g., the metrical count. It can only be poetry because it has a diction that maneuvers it into the sound of poetry. There's no other proof or other claim it can have.

The four books of *Gunslinger* were written rather consecutive but they took a long time because I had other things to do about that time—I had to make a living for a new and growing family. These were troublesome times.

I associate book 2 with the tone of Chicago actually. This is the Chicago book. And it's rather quieting. It's rather desperate. And so it's got all of that time suddenly.

This is after the first flush of "Wow! I'm really onto something. And I, you know, I'm going to make a metaphysical cowboy and is the world ready for this and, whoa!" And suddenly after I finished it I thought, "Yeah, the world's ready for this, and it should get a lot better." You know, it's got to. And so book 2 reflects that. This was, I'm talking about, 1971, just before Nixon got it. The war was already getting everybody's nerves up, you know. It's a pretty desperate place. Things are not fine. Chicago is still remembered as this place where the peaceniks got elbowed out of the way. That atmosphere's still got a lot of charge, although it has been three years already. It's reflected in the address to citizens, a certain growing contempt. You ask a question and you get: "Do you really want to ask that question because I'd really like to answer." There's a lot of that kind of stuff going on. So book 2 is very influenced by that. That's all tone.

But the theoretical tone? This book was not invented in that way. It's just, to me, this is anthropology. This is just Lévi-Strauss living in Chicago.

Student: I notice that each book is published separately. Did you conceive of the whole work in its entirety?

Dorn: The cast moves. It continues along the stage like a serial. I grew up on pre-TV serials, and the pre-TV continuity was the serial; like when you went down and had your dime for the show and the rest for a bag of popcorn, you got a serial. You got a couple of movies. You got a lot for your dime. That was all you needed. That was Saturday, and when you left, you could come back. You were free for the rest of the week.

So this is a serial of very different time. This is a book. This is a war book. This is a Vietnam War book traveling by old methods to get them some time to talk, in order to make a social condition in which their conversation can be ranging.

It's got a lot of drugs in it because drugs were actually the air you breathed. They were substantial. Drugs were important. It was the beginning of the drug war.

It's only now coming out that the CIA ran crack into black ghettos in Los Angeles. Back then the CIA was doing something rather more heinous: sewing kilos of heroin inside the thorax of the cadavers of our returning dead from Vietnam, sewing it back up, and shipping the body back to Long Beach, San Francisco, and Chicago. These were the first containers of the heroin.

In book 2, when I becomes "the container of the thing it contains"—this is a reference to using our returning dead as containers. This is where they really got them. This was Burmese heroin, just like it is now. This was Air America. This was the first big off-the-books money.

So, yes, drugs are in the book, as Marge Perloff points out in her introduction. She's done her drugs too. But the Gunslinger reference is financial as well. It does refer to the Zurich gunslingers who were at that time messing with the market. These people were anonymous way before Michael Milken, you know, the guy who stripped America of its absolute fortune and did three years for it. These were the precursors of Milken. But with the Swiss, well, you could barely hear a tick. To some, there's something about Americans that is so vulgar that when they steal a hundred billion dollars, they really want you to know it. They bang the gong saying, "This is what I got away with, man, I just like robbed them—the pension funds of like a half million people last night before I went to bed. It's better than sex."

I assume everybody who's riding a Lexus down the street had a piece of a savings and loan. I assume it. Where else did it come from? I assume I'm paying for that. I assume I'm making the payments on it. Except there are no payments on it because they paid cash. I'm making the payments on it. And when you get jobs and that'll make you happy, you'll be paying for it too.

Was your question more formal?

Student: Well, yeah, actually.

Dorn: They're in train. It's an array. It's just a serial. And it's really "sixty—late sixties, early seventies." And a period in the mid-seventies when I was able to work more than I usually can. So several books got done at that time. Then there's "The Cycle," which is a skaldic piece, a kind of mimic; not the rhyme, the rhyme is very eccentric. But the form is visually skaldic—the four lines, and its procedure, the way it talks is skaldic. And I wanted that to be very northern, not even European but North Atlantic, Icelandic.

Why? To pay homage to that freebooterism and the kind of nonstructured, nonenslaving invasion of the New World, say totally unlike the Spanish. The Vikings were simply coming to raid, and were very much in the spirit of Howard Hughes, who was an early primitive kind of raider. He didn't raid like Michael Milken and those people, because they were just wire artists. Howard Hughes was old-fashioned in the sense that he thought even if it was crooked, you should still make it. You should still earn it, even if it's criminal, you should still earn it. These people like Boesky, they were just strippers. The late postmodern people, they just like wire it to themselves. They'd buy a company and wire all the assets to themselves. They're amazing, and very postmodern American. In that sense Howard Hughes was old-fashioned.

So, he is the kind of male muse that runs through this. He was an early Ted Turner type. He inherited a smallish, twenty-five-million-dollar fortune, which was quite a bit in his day but still not one of the great fortunes, based on the Cobra bit his old man invented, a Houston fortune of oil people. He won the proprietary rights to something like the Cobra bit, which was a very fine drilling bit. That's what he started with.

Hughes went to Hollywood. He married, yet he didn't marry anybody, actually. He did the equivalent of dozens of Jane Fondas. He bought a studio. He was a director, sometimes great, sometimes bad, but he didn't care. He bought RKO. He took a tour, and as he was leaving in his limousine, somebody said, "Well, what would you like us to do, Mr. Hughes," and he looked back and he said, "Paint it." Fantastic guy. And also totally insane, maybe one of the most obsessive hypochondriacs who ever lived. The symbolism of increasingly needing Kleenex boxes is weird. I mean walking around without house shoes but Kleenex boxes. And him ordering Kleenex by the case and he would use like maybe, oh, fifteen to twenty boxes of Kleenex a day! Really. When he would move into a hotel, he would clear everybody out. He'd move into the top floor and everybody would have go. He'd buy the building and throw them out. That's the whole thing about how he moved.

> Right, boy
> They say he moved to Vegas
> or bought Vegas and
> moved it.

He had a sense of humor with vast money. Whereas now I'm afraid there doesn't seem to be any indication that billionaires have got any sense of humor. They're not funny. Bill Gates is not funny. He's sort of funny but he doesn't mean to be funny.

Student: And Ross Perot?

Dorn: Yeah, that's a good extension actually. He's a strange one. Perot is the first government-created billionaire. All his money came from government contracts. He didn't *make* anything ever.

All his money comes from government contracts. All of it. He has no money in stocks, by the way. He's a total bond guy. He makes nothing, whereas Howard Hughes created things: Trans World Airlines, the Hughes Tool Company till the end, he made movies. This was very old-fashioned. Ross Perot makes nothing except money, and that's not actually money, that's just paper money. Our new billionaires insist that we keep the printing presses going night and day to supply them with their billions because it's just paper. How this is not read as inflation I have never been able to understand. The right wing now says that we don't have to honor contracts because they're not real. That dollar bill is no better than the dollar bill that I could print at home. It's the same thing. They're printing those things. I've got just as much a right to do that as the government does. This is basically what's going on.

So Ross, as they call him in Texarcana, he's not like Milken, although Milken was a stripper—an asset stripper. He worked hard and he is brilliant. But his brains are in his ears. That's how he works: he just hears about money and gets it.

Howard Hughes was one of the great moguls actually, the first of his kind because they had the telegraph, which was the first wire. And money got fast with the telegraph. Unlike Jay Gould or Uncle Daniel Drew, Hughes was a pilot. He was modern.

Actually all these terms apply to Michael Milken and Levy and Ivan Boesky, then known as the Russian. They're all post-modern because they're all computerized. The stock market crash of '29 was a crash of margins—people extended the margin because that was like speculation on credit and suddenly nobody had any money. Everybody tries to collect with everything else. That was one crash. That's when everybody defenestrated, and that was a crash. But then the crash of '87 was the crash of the machine, and anybody who's had a computer that's crashed knows about that.

On the technical problems setting up to write a long poem in which there's going to be a cast and they're going to talk, and so forth, you need to think about how you're going to operate that right off. Obviously in a poem of this kind of skepticism, you're going to need quotation marks to satisfy that language as a signal to the reader that this is in quotation marks. So that, even though it's not a play, it is dramatic, only not with mere dramatic dialogue, but a multilogue.

Once you abandon the quotation marks and the absolute direct signal, you've got to make it clear to the reader who's talking. It really comes down to using some archaics like "saith" or, inventing, to get around "said," signals that so-and-so are talking. But when the exchanges are fairly rapid and follow on each other, then I just let that take care of itself. There are lots of different kinds of ways of proceeding.

But *Gunslinger* is not an epic. The idea that this was going to be the kind of a long trip of an epic-like structure is an awfully difficult thing to claim because we know epics as archaic, hairy-chested sorts of things. That's got another implication. All those things are difficult at this point.

In '76, *Gunslinger* was called experimental, when it's actually not. It's really just an attempt to meditate what there is left of the available instrument. It's not an epic, but it's going to work that kind of trip. When people started "tripping" in the sixties, those weren't epic trips. There was that problem. *Gunslinger* reflects this in the struggle to make it that kind of a book.

I did learn something about the Western mentality and the modern; the fact that you get a series of population dumpings, really. England was always an exporting island. It's a vigorous people in a very small space. So they exported a population, just like the Mexicans are doing now. I call that population dumping, but let's just call it "exporting the population." The westward expansion was exporting surplus population again.

Well, everything's tied down here—"We own all these properties, so why don't you get going? Here's a wagon and a horse. See you later."

People who went west didn't necessarily want to go west. They couldn't have all wanted to go west. People starved, they got diseases, they lost their children. Going west was no piece of cake, really. Going west was no flapjack.

I was really influenced by the spaghetti Westerns, the Italian films made in the early sixties and early Clint Eastwood films. He's very impressive in those. The way the Italians took the western formula, and I read that as Virgilian, and not Homeric. I read that as Roman and I tried to very consciously follow that flight. This was modern.

The whole thing about *The Aeneid* was that the people weren't like Achilles. Achilles said, "Yeah, bring them on," like the super-est dude who ever lived. But by the time you get to *The Aeneid*, I mean, they're not so sure they want to do this.

The difference between those two epics is immense. Suddenly with Virgil, it's Western. The first Western expansion was from Athens to Rome, then to the Iberian Peninsula. Regarding the Mediterranean being the whole world is so Italian. Athens is their New York. Rome is their San Francisco.

The two myths operate like that, and we're still actually very much operating within the confines of this. It's one of the great losses of the present prejudices in education that we've repudiated that inheritance, because those two epics are still extremely instructive to our present problems. People who don't know those epics are unable to assess a great deal. They don't know. They're not instantly on the ground with an analysis of what's going on. If you haven't read *The Odyssey*, well, it would be as if you didn't know about the wheel. You might think that a Goodyear radial is a great big black Life Saver. But when you know *The Odyssey* and *The Aeneid* well, you can read everything because those two were the initial readings. Those were *the* readings. They still are.

Abhorrences concerning the State of American Poetry

In 1984, as Ronald Reagan steamrolled toward reelection, Ed Dorn began "Abhorrences," a daybook of running commentary on the atrocities he witnessed in the press. Abhorrences exemplifies Dorn's poetics of aggression. The combined effect of these statemental lyrics or op-ed poems is a broadside attack against political and cultural trends in the United States. Dorn became less tolerant of such intellectual fashions of the day as multiculturalism, Language poetry, the American academic sycophancy for all things French and theoretical, and the ascendancy of literary genres that he saw as devoid of meaning and content precisely when the times demanded clarity and synthesis.

In this talk at the Workshop Line National Series in Detroit, Michigan, May 24, 1984, Dorn describes the process and context of early Abhorrences, and he delivers a brief caustic tirade of the sort his students remember from that decade.

Initially, to forewarn you: what I have to say is not really organized. It had something to do with my own present practice and dissatisfaction with what I read in the world of poetry, and my attempt to do something else in the meantime—to construct a kind of commentary sentence structure which will hold a thought that comes from just living in the world, hearing what people are telling me, and hearing what other creatures, who I don't immediately recognize as people, are telling me.

It mostly comes from the news. I'm writing a series of commentaries called "Abhorrences" that derives mainly from a certain kind of rhetoric I'm reading. And I'm not using "rhetoric" in the spirit that the word was used in the late sixties, which was to put down anybody who was making sense, but rather as it was practiced as an art mainly in the eighteenth century by people like Sydney Smith, a kind of early nineteenth-century, late-eighteenth-century divine, a very fat guy actually, who, according to most judgments and standards today would be considered totally loathsome. I think he was one of the great writers of the period, not because of the ideas he held necessarily, but because of the way he expressed them.

In my advancing age, I've learned that most ideas are essentially dumb but endlessly repeated. I get more interested in how they're fashioned rather than what they're meant to express, because they really don't change that much. In fact, they don't say that much, as they are often the product of a certain kind of vested interest with ample doses of euphemism, neologism, and plain stupidity trying to circumvent *real* meaning because real meaning seems no longer tolerable.

To take a recent case, for instance, the present mindless fight that's going on about aid to El Salvador. Jesse Helms, that regrettable and highness (a "right-wing-nut" as Ed Sanders would say), did point out that President Ronald Reagan bought the election in El Salvador, effectively installing Napoleon Duarte. Duarte didn't speak like anybody in the United States Congress had heard before—like a sincere gentleman, but a man presumably in quite a lot of trouble. But he bowled over Congress and got the money. So, in a certain sense Jesse Helms is right. Reagan did buy the election. Yet this is supposed to be the model for democracy in an open society? Roberto D'Aubiusson is not an abnormal character in the area he comes from; in fact, he may be a lot more normal than Duarte. He's complaining that the election was bought and he's correct too.

There's a certain kind of mentality that refuses to recognize these things. These are kinds of things that poetry ought to inspect.

I don't see poetry today talking about anything at all. When it purports to talk about something, it's talking about the extremely questionable ideas, if such things can be attributed, of various writers who will remain forever adolescent and novice and who have no real interest in the language. They have a kind of interest in a kind of linguistic leeching which has come to be called LANGUAGE. One of the first things they do is say, "I'm famous." which is then instantly true. The value of that assertion (and it's okay as an assertion—you can say you're anything) is very questionable, precisely because the language is empty. And I think the language is empty in part due to the militantly regressive stand against language being rational. I'm not saying it's got anything to do with, you know, rhyme or reason in that orthodox sense, but its inability to acknowledge anything exterior to itself is probably one of its most virulent diseases.

I don't think prose is in quite that sort of emergency state. Mere prose psychology is always more or less more legitimate. This derives from the fact that prose takes another kind of concentration. If poetry is a concentration of attention or the reduction of attention to its possible essence, prose is a concentration on how things really are. Poetry has never been under obligation to say what things really are. And I don't think it ever ought to be.

Nevertheless, at the present moment people tend to be more interested in what things really are than how we can imagine them because, while our imaginations have become more active, they're useless, they're less valued. So a lot more people have and operate within what used to be called an imagination. Before, imagination was kind of a profession. People who had imagination were expected to exercise that. They were paid to do it and in fact it was good work for a fair service and there was nothing wrong with it.

When, on the other hand, the personal preoccupation also includes a kind of self-demand at the exclusion of other demands, then imagination gets distorted in that respect, and that's what's now going on. One's self-gratification and self-preoccupation and concern for the demands of the personal have become so preponderant that it's become almost impossible actually to listen to what anybody has to say about anything, and I would include what I'm saying now to all of you.

This training has gone on for certainly ten, probably fifteen, and possibly twenty years. It's created interesting prose. It hasn't created interesting poetry.

In order to clear the decks, and really go back and get it all out of the way, so that we can work ourselves again into what might once again be called poetry, because poetry *is* real, that would be to reinspect the properties of the sentence.

This is my operating notion in my own work now—writing sentences which turn out to be extremely brief essays. Commentary is probably another description of it. And it's very dry. It's not necessarily flat, but it's very dry. I think that's the place to re-begin as we shuffle our way to the end of this fairly boring century, in spite of all its upheaval.

One of the problems of the twentieth century of course is that it mirrors in so many ways the nineteenth century. The end of this century which is upon us gets to look a lot like the end of the nineteenth. One of its losses is that its ambition for de-generacy, its ambition for wholesale aesthetic waste, its ambition for self-regarding demagoguery, really fell short of the mark. That's one of the deep psychological disappointments of the fin de siècle that we're undergoing. It's traumatic.

That was also true of the late Victorians, to a certain extent, although they had rather more rectitude than we have, and at least one overriding virtue, which is that they were rather more private about it. As it turned out, that was wasted effort on their part because the academic industry in our century has done nothing but irritate them and excavate them and turn them into a weird piece of archaeology. We've giving the Victorians no rest at all. There's nothing more popular than a preoccupa-tion with the Victorians because it gets turned into patting our-selves on the back, that we're so damned superior, and that they were so fucked up. That's really essentially what the academic industry is up to. And people are getting jobs on this now. To my mind, it's an empty, useless subject, and in one hundred years time it will be seen as one of the major strategic mistakes of intellectual labor of this period: to have been so stupid as to have been preoccupied with the Victorians.

And another thing I'm really getting sick and tired of is this eternal, unexpected presumption, which has only increased in our century and among our people, of the inviolable truths of the Vienna school of psychology.

If you want to talk about banning the competition, like when a city like Detroit limits the number of Japanese car imports, that's nothing compared to the Freudian's putting up tariff bar-riers to other ideas and its blatantly squeezing out other ideas.

Freudianism really only applies to a very small society, a very privileged society, in one town in central Europe in one period who had a very particular set of hang-ups. I never saw it apply to anybody else, but it's been presumed that it applies to the entire world. That perpetuates this preoccupation with the pseudo-analysis that goes on with late-Victorian life. Most of that motivation, in fact, does come from Vienna. It's the same thing as, say, a white man walking down the street and feeling guilty about black people, when that white man never in his life occupied a southern plantation, never owned a slave, never passed any of the legislation, never attended a lynching, never did any of those things, and yet participates in a culture in which his whole mental apparatus and emotional system is abrogated by a kind of pseudo-inherited guilt for a lot of other people that he didn't even know. I see the application of Freudian principles in much that light—engulfing people and essentially distracting them, curbing their potential thought and unfortunately not curbing their appetites, though.

One of the things that's really bad about this period is that everybody's waiting around to be a great writer, and, you know, that just doesn't happen. You have to write a lot to get great writing, let alone great writers. And who cares if there are great writers? It's the activity and the energy and the perception and the incisiveness and the cognition of writing that elevates the reader's mind, not whether it's written by a great writer. Who cares? It's up to the people one hundred years hence to determine whether the writing was great or not—just like we inspect one hundred years back. So it's not up to us. I think one of the biggest fallacies of the present moment is that we're so anxious to judge the quality of what's going on now instead of doing it.

A good case is Jack Kerouac. There's a bunch of numbskulls who, you know, "Oh, Jack Kerouac, isn't it too bad he's dead, we could still go on the road if he wasn't. We could destroy our livers if he was still around." And so they put him in all kinds of positions which were not true to him and they write false books like Gerald Nicosia's for instance. It's the cheapest kind of trading on an essentially fucked-up, but also essentially noble, man's life. That is an indication of how low this period has sunk, actually. It's really just too quick. That is the point I was trying to get to. It's like, if we are enamored of Jack Kerouac's work, read him, do that, and let it rest at that. But the judgments that are now forthcoming about what "Beat" meant are totally empty and supercilious and gratuitous and disgusting, as far as I'm concerned.

Kerouac's a good example of a character who to a certain extent invited it. But on the other hand I think it would be a good mark of this period if it resisted the invitation, and I don't see that happening. In fact, I don't see this period resisting any invitation.

Student: Earlier you talked about Language poets as writing without external referent, without a referent to outside, you know, as if somehow maybe that meant they could write language that didn't refer to outside. I wondered if you couldn't see the Language writers as somehow prophetic of your current writing practice, making sentences, as a new kind of practice. I saw that you weren't willing to call it poetry, precisely. I mean, I know you were doing it before, but can't you see that, however boring, Language school certainly polarized a lot of poets and made them go back, as I thought yesterday, to the libraries and rethink language, and a system of language, and how things meant things, and things like that. Sure I'm more interested in your writing than the Language poets, and I have always have been. But, Ed, are you really a Language poet?

Dorn: If I were a vindictive man, that would be a dangerous thing to say. But actually I wasn't referring to the Language poets. I was speaking much more in general than that. I think they're one manifestation of what you're describing. You see, I don't necessarily buy the idea that the root to connection with humanity at large is through the self. I think that the networks and webs between us that we set up in fact [are] external. And I believe this nurtures the internal so that we all then have that internal thing that we can share. However I don't think that it's generated or constructed or made out of the relation of our personal experience.

Now the exceptions to that are great. They're wholesale almost. You know, if you want to speak particularly about people who have concentrated on themselves as a projection of the mass. But again I don't think that that's really the main stem of the industry of writing actually. I'm encouraged by the very small and so far relatively, compared to, say, the eighteenth century, rebirth and regeneration of the essay and the essayist. I think poetry can benefit a lot from that practice.

I also don't think that there is any deep connection between poetry and what's poetic necessarily. As we know, there's an awful lot of capability in prose without running the risk of being poetic, which is said to destroy it. There's still a lot of poetry in prose, which is not damaging to it. All of these distinctions have to be made kind of constantly and instantaneously as we talk about them.

I'm not talking exactly about the Language school, and in fact, I don't know that much about the Language school. Practically everything I know about the Language school has been taught to me by a man who's entirely prejudiced against the Language school—Tom Clark, who's a man I pay a lot of attention to, actually because his fervor is quite believable. By the way, his new book on Jack Kerouac, which is in the Harcourt Brace Jovanovich new series of picture biographies, is an extremely dry and keen analysis of all the sort of mistakes that have been made in past biographies. It's a really handsome and readable book. He's really very traditionalist in a way that I'm not: his whole background, his education at Ann Arbor at the time that he received it, and in his subsequent finishing off of that education at Cambridge. In spite of how he looks and how people may feel about him, he is quite traditional. Clark's education in the history and the practice of English literature past is very orthodox actually.

One of his objections, as I understand it, and I would certainly agree with this, is to the attention and surrounding preoccupation with what poetry is. Prose doesn't preoccupy itself with what it is nearly as much as poetry does. And that's also always been true.

Like Clark, I don't also have much patience with the French tendency to pretend that you can analyze something that's not there. Structuralism, deconstructionism, semiotics, the whole language analysis business puts me to sleep pretty much. Anybody who's read those people must instantly recognize what pop cultural analysis it is; the same that goes on in journalism, as much as it does, goes on in philosophy, or linguistic philosophy, if it's a philosophy. There's so much of it going on that it generates its own clichés so swiftly that it's like talking inside a barrel.

I can read [Claude] Lévi-Strauss with more profit simply because he's so exhaustive in his information that there's a value in it. What he makes of that information I find it possible really to ignore. For my purposes, I'm not really that interested in the end product of what he thinks. If it supplies a base for his thinking, then I always find that interesting. Historical method still satisfies my purposes much more.

A couple of years ago, I got real interested in the Colin McCabe case. He was a structuralist critic, an authority on Godard, who was denied tenure at Cambridge University. It was in the British newspapers quite a bit. I happened to get transcripts of the Cambridge Senate proceedings on his case, which was a very elegantly printed document of about eighty pages of the speeches made pro and con for his case. Somebody should reprint it, because on this question, it's really the best document. People stood up in the Senate at Cambridge and spoke for and against Colin McCabe. Christopher Ricks waffled because he didn't want to appear chauvinistic, but his dedication to the historical method is rather complete. It's great to hear where people think their bread and butter's at, as displayed in their arguments for and against this man. I'm not saying that Colin McCabe himself is right, wrong, indifferent, or anything. But the attitude toward his stand and the English establishment suddenly closing ranks and saying, "We're not going to let this evil French thing into our medieval precinct" is one of the most interesting things I've ever read.

Student: What you were saying about rhetoric I thought was interesting because you looked not toward this century but to the nineteenth century, to feed your poetry with rhetoric, the sentence and sentence structures, instead of things like structuralism.

Dorn: As a method, I could be totally wrong on all of this. I don't know how interesting my poetry is. To me, it's just something I've got to do, and I want to do it that way now. In a year and a half or two years if I'm, you know, writing and sentient at all, I might be drawing on something else.

But in the first place, it seems inconceivable to me that there could be anything like content in structuralism. It's the opposite of content. But in terms of how you can dispose thought along a line with all the commas implied, or how to fashion language is what I get out of various rhetorical practices in the past.

Rhetoric, the word itself, as a neologism of the late sixties and early seventies, simply meant somebody who was trying to deceive you when they were talking to you. That, hence, "That's just a bunch of rhetoric," right? That's not what I'm saying. That use of the word in fact has already passed. I mean. It passed with "relevance."

Student: So you see things returning back. Instead of Language poets breaking up syntax, do you see things returning to the commas and the way that the grammar is placed?

Dorn: No, I don't. I see me returning to it. I don't see them returning to it. Their urge to break up syntax and to destroy meaning is only an attempt to hide a lack of idea-making or idea-having or idea-generation.

Student: A lot of French feministic psychoanalysts, like Julia Kristeva, say that the reason that they break up syntax is to destroy phallocentric discourse.

Dorn: Yes, and they also say another reason is to destroy the authority of the syntax. I understand that, and in fact I appreciate the fact that women want to destroy authority. I don't wholly disagree with that, in fact. It's just that the authority or let's say the tyranny, which always occupies a vacuum in authority, disturbs me also. And I don't believe, necessarily, that alternative systems have to prove themselves viable in order to replace the system that they're replacing, and that's been a common human experience for a long, long time. In one way or another that's happening every day. But what's increasingly happening is that it's being replaced with nothing. It has the flaws of any other kind of anarchy.

Student: Okay. I just want to take that a little step further and I'm not sure that you can say Kristeva or [Luce] Irigaray know about people in this country, but I think they might be interested to know that in America up until a certain point on the poetic line of the left, if you want to call it that, you find mostly men. Then all of a sudden, beyond that point, there comes to the fore a lot of women and many of them share this one thing of breaking down the syntax and producing something else in its place. I don't see this as anarchy. Naming names might make it clear what they share; say Maureen Owen, Bernadette Mayer, Alice Notley, Kathleen Fraser, and maybe add Kathy Acker for other reasons. They all seem to share that.

Dorn: Well, what is it, though? I don't understand.

Student: It's what they produce under discourse; that is, attuned to women's needs to write a poetry of the women.

Student: Well, you said that you're not as interested in the ideas that poetry puts forth, but in the forms—in the way it expresses it, not what it expresses?

Dorn: Well, I am in fact interested in the ideas in poetry, and actually less in the form at the present moment. Until the revival of rhyme and meter, which is bound to happen, ideas are in ascendance over form. But I don't see ideas really being generated out of broken syntax because I consider that aphasic and is totally reactionary. The late New Critics, for instance, in the fifties were analyzing poetry mainly on that basis. Most of that came out of the Prague school. I don't know how much historically you know about this but there's a whole library on this question.

Alice Notley I like, not because she's broken up the syntax but because she titillates my mind in a mild way and I think she's funny. But I would never go to her to learn anything. I mean, she just gives me pleasure that has always been one of the functions of language. But it's not the only function of language. And I don't think it's actually the only function of women, either. I like a lot of women who talk in straight syntactical form, and don't break anything up, and in fact don't even give me pleasure.

Genderism, as it's now come to be called (yet the latest neologism), is in desperate search for the home for the mind of a woman. That's not only legitimate, but a necessary pursuit. However, there's no way that I think the precepts of the Language school or any antisyntactical, discontinuous discourse is any better way to do that than half a dozen other ways that might be pursued, and, in fact are being pursued.

Germaine Greer has just written a very reactionary book on marriage and the family called *Sex and Destiny: The Politics of Human Fertility* (1984). Fay Weldon has just written a book, a series of letters as if to her daughter who's reading Jane Austen. It's a very interesting discussion of the mind of Jane Austen. Women are going to read that. That's an altogether different kind of practice than experimental writing theory of any kind.

Student: In talking about different aspects of an essay, if you're returning to the sentence and the grammatical structure, do you return to the narrative then also? Does the idea make sense in the kind of narrative way that everything leads down to another thing?

Dorn: I do have a lot of respect for narrative. I think it's a basic human method. I'm using the word *essay,* as applied to the short poems in *Abhorrences* now, not essay like by [Michel] Montaigne, but more in the sense of a kind of expanded aphorism. In other words, it would be composed of several sentences instead of maybe one.

All of these things, like "narrative" and "consecutive" and so forth, that I have a feeling you're proposing as frightening, I'm not frightened by. I think there's a universe of illumination inside that, unless I've really missed it somewhere. I don't consider that threatening. Furthermore, it would have to be explained to me, by you or somebody else, how narrative is threatening, or tied to a kind of patriarchal dominance or something.

Student: Well, I just find that your ideas are a little different than what I've been reading lately.

Dorn: Well, sure. My ideas are not only not fashionable, but they're not even current. I know what you're saying. I'm saying something else. I'm saying that whatever else poetry can do, and it has many functions even including certain of the best. I'm not excluding any of the functions of that practice. My concern is more with what traditionally poetry has attempted to say. In other words, that the poetic is the height of language, whether it's in poetry, or all the various kinds of prose that we can think of, including journalism. I don't know of a poem of the last couple of decades that has risen above an intensity, for instance, of Hunter Thompson's *Fear and Loathing* essay. I don't think that's a threat to poetry. Poetry is where you find it, not where it says that it's at. Where it says it's at, I don't find a lot of poetry there—very often, mostly none.

Student: It seems to be, well, I guess from Tom Clark being so, well, against the Language school and the Language school being against everyone else, there seems to be sort of a segregation of groups of people. Am I right?

Dorn: I know what you mean. Again in defense of Tom Clark, he's going to turn out to be the most valuable virus a lot of people ever encountered because, unless the Language school is entirely witless, which is a possibility, they can only profit by his attack, just like Allen Ginsberg and Buddhists in general in this country should have profited by *The Great Naropa Poetry Wars*.

One of the problems here is people's overwhelming ignorance. They don't know enough about the history of writing. For instance, anybody who knew about Grub Street, for instance, during the years 1725–1775 when it flourished, would have recognized Tom Clark's function immediately, and wouldn't have given it two thoughts—they would have said, "Ah, that's it. That's that. This is recurring again." But a lot of people said, "Oh, my God, what's this guy doing? What's he trying to do to us?"

Student: So you see the arguments as being healthy?

Dorn: Absolutely. One of the reasons why language is so sick now and cliché-ridden and lame and boring and laid-out, and about to go to sleep, is because there aren't a thousand Tom Clarks.

If I were writing a prescription right now, you know, if I had my shiny thing here, a stethoscope around my neck, that's the prescription I'd write. Take one thousand Tom Clarks before going to bed.

Student: I have a question about the medicine before I swallow it. The last page of *The Great Naropa Poetry Wars* is a list of people who were paid off by Ron Padgett and Lyn Hejinian and Michael Palmer. They pay off all these Trungpa clones? Yeah, right. And in the list of the Trungpa clones are all these people like Lewis Warsh and Bernadette Mayer who never would give a penny to a Buddhist. I always found that to be a bunch of lies, that last page. The rest of the book, I thought, was really good, but that last page seemed to me as just a bunch of hogwash. And why was that last page put on there? Am I supposed to believe that Ron Padgett was working for Trungpa Rinpoche? If you're going to be an investigative reporter, why not tell the truth?

Dorn: I don't think it's a matter of telling the truth. I think when you swallow the toad, you swallow the warts. People go too far, and Tom Clark's human. By the time he got there, he probably wanted to do the whole bit and just put that last page in there. I'm not prepared to argue the aesthetic propriety of any of this. I'm just saying that its use is very clear to me, and it's healthy, and the lack of it is very unhealthy.

Student: I've noticed how we've started talking about sentences and now we're talking about money and it feels like Pound to me.

When Pound was looking around in the twenties and thirties and trying to figure out why it was that people, both poets and other kinds of writers, didn't seem to have a language available to them that would allow them to be accurate, at least in Pound's terms, the way that Pound thought about it, as we know, sent him off into economics and money and who had control of certain kinds of language and who didn't, and I'm wondering about the extent to which you're getting involved in these concerns about sentences in your writing, or whether there's a way that you've found that you can just bracket that material and leave it for somebody else. As you can see, it's a question that isn't very well formed, but maybe you have a response to it.

Dorn: The way that I understand what you're saying, however unannotated and inert, is really a message to another mind. I don't have economic theories, actually. My closest thing to proposing an economic model would just be some kind of co-operative society, that is what it would boil down to, as against one in which a small number of people have the upper hand on exploiting the others. That's not to say very much because everybody more or less feels that way, unless they've got the upper hand, then they don't feel that way.

In any case, I don't really feel that polemical about it. Aesthetically, my hope for language is that it is transmittable and that other intelligences can use it. In the meantime, since there are such wide swaths of bullshit being laid down now, it can behoove the small poem to be as piercing and arrow-like and to the point as possible. You see I don't believe in a broken syntax any more than I believe in a broken arrow.

Student: Is this skeptical? Do you deny that you can communicate effectively by destructing syntax?

Dorn: No, I don't deny that. We do it all the time in speech. Some of that speech is effective. Some of the most interesting and enlightening conversations I've ever had in fact have been with crazy persons who habitually speak in abrupted syntax. The difference with speech is that, as a transmission, it is so much older and rooted in an archaic system of perception that we carry with us than any kind of writing is. To me, that's a different world. It's a different world of attention. I pay a different attention to that. It's an altogether different fascination.

When that goes on in writing, unless there's a certain kind of brilliance of vocabulary or some redeeming feature, I get irritated. I'll put up with anything anybody says to me; literally anything. But if they write something that I have trouble with or I've got to make allowances for, or if I've got to fill in the spaces somehow, or I've got to guess, or I've got to do anything really, it irritates me. I tend to drop it. I don't want to waste my time that way. I've got a certain limited amount of time as we all do on earth, and I'll invariably choose to spend it another way.

Student: Then why do you admire the writing of Tom Raworth if that kind of syntax is so irritating?

Dorn: Uh, because it's not like that.

Student: It's not like what?

Dorn: Raworth's syntax is rather continuous. You've got to remember that's a foreign language, which is important. His leaps are intellectual leaps, not really syntactical leaps. Any close inspection, and that would also go for a lot of good, but extremely unspectacular and therefore not popular poets writing in England, like say Jeremy Prynne, who is according to the way you've described it, even more disrupted, but it's mental. I don't mean that the way the English use that to mean crazy. It's like . . . not mental. Let's see, what is it? It's . . . well, maybe one could say intellectual, I suppose.

But they're not called Language poets, and for a good reason. Because the Language poets would be disgusted if they read those people. It would be even more disrupted than they have even conceived, and they would turn to dust with envy.

Interview at Madison

Ed Dorn visited the University of Wisconsin at Madison after the Reagan landslide victory in November 1984 and presented more "Insufferances, Intolerances, and Abhorrences: The Politics of Poetry in Our Time."

In an interview conducted after the public event on November 19, 1984, and later published in "Contemporary Literature" (vol. 27, no. 1, 1986), Tandy Sturgeon teases out the ideological underpinnings of Dorn's intellectual formation and his satire. She focuses the poet on a few short pieces from "Hello La Jolla" and "Yellow Lola" (1980), poems that Donald Wesling aptly refers to as Dorn's statemental lyrics, as his "Abhorrences" (1990) may also quite well be described.

Tandy Sturgeon: I take it that you feel the connections made between you and the Black Mountain School are overblown.

Edward Dorn: The reality was great. The subsequent history of what it was has been extremely confused, and not very interesting for the most part. There are some things that just don't yield to a constant rehash. What was really exciting about Black Mountain was being there. I think that if you're reviewing an exciting event, like, say, Waterloo, or any war, actually, it's probably a lot more interesting than an educational experience. An educational experience doesn't tend to be that exciting, at least not very often.

Sturgeon: You have to do your work.

Dorn: Of course. The interest in Black Mountain was not so much to impart what it was able to do for the individual in terms of enlightenment, but the gossip about what it was as a social organism—which was much less significant than its pedagogical function.

Sturgeon: Do you think it's at all useful to know all the Black Mountain gossip, to study it? Do you think it's usable gossip?

Dorn: I think gossip is nice and scandal's even better. But that's something you have to make for yourself—feeding off other gossip is terrible.

Sturgeon: That's true, and yet the published and publicized quarrels writers have, which can be categorized as gossip, are apparently quite attractive to readers. I'm thinking as much of Dryden and Pope as of the word-slinging that goes on in *American Book Review, Sulfur, Exquisite Corpse, Rolling Stock,* and other "mainstream" literary reviews. Why do you think readers enjoy this so much?

Dorn: Readers enjoy it because that's one of the best sides of literature. Writers love to fight and whine. They all basically hate each other. Friendship among writers is just a total pretense.

Sturgeon: And yet their fallings-out seem much more dramatic than genuine. Look at Norman Mailer and Gore Vidal, for example. What about you? Do you have any enemies?

Dorn: I don't have any enemies, no. I don't have any serious enemies. It's hard to have serious enemies now, this is not a heavy time.

Sturgeon: Would you like to have serious enemies?

Dorn: Oh for sure! The thing is, Mailer and Vidal and Capote are high-society writing. That's a very different thing, that's professional fighting.

Sturgeon: Would that make Pope's *Dunciad* high-society writing?

Dorn: Pope was a great fighter. He generated revulsion and disgust and dissension just to amuse himself, and made capital out of it. *The Dunciad, The Art of Sinking*—they're masterpieces of that whole genre. That's an art, really, and writers just love it—after all, there's not much profit otherwise.

Sturgeon: You're suggesting, then, that it's a way writers can receive a profit?

Dorn: Well, what profit they get.

Sturgeon: And that's not necessarily a negative statement?

Dorn: No, it's not.

Sturgeon: Your discussion the other night at your reading, which had to do with the problems of so-called "political" poetry, focused on a redefinition of what politics really is in this context. To your remarks I would add a comment of Eliot Weinberger's, from a recent review of Carolyn Forche's *The Country Between Us* in *Sulfur:* "To presume to link arms, declaring oneself equal to those who have endured such torment, to speak to people who will be corpses in the morning and claim that you too are digging deeper into your own death . . . is more than naiveté and audacity. It is the liberal side of colonialism." This is of course in response to attitudes commonly held by North American writers toward Central and South American situations. How, in your opinion, does one maintain a legitimate political stance as a North American poet?

Dorn: Well, I assume everybody's going to be dead in the morning. You see, the point for me here is the simple fact that sensibility is no substitute for consciousness. And I think that's the main problem. Either we define our allegiances to certain honorific aspects of human nature or we don't. Most of us know all the time that politics in poetry really amounts to enunciation. Politics in politics amounts to subterfuge, obscurantism, and hiding all you can. But that's politics in politics, not politics in writing. Because there's no power in politics in writing, except enunciation. The registration is there and that's all there is to it.

Sturgeon: There's another direction you've taken that I'm curious about: your decision to become a part of the academy, to be a professor of English. Do you think that there are limitations or sacrifices involved in this decision, in respect to either writing or teaching? Your own background at Black Mountain makes me wonder where you would "send" a young person for whom you have educational responsibility.

Dorn: Well, I don't think you "send" anybody to get that experience. People who are lucky enough to encounter a forming process come onto it themselves. It's difficult to say that there's somebody that they can go to, because the really meaningful event is that they discover the person who becomes their fertilizer. A lot of people don't get that, and yet they get along as well as anybody else. I feel rather complexly about teaching, actually. It doesn't affect my writing, because I keep that separate. I teach to make my living. It's a legitimate living. I've always worked at one job or another, but I've never worked at writing in that sense. For instance, Richard Brautigan, no matter what you think of his writing, was a pure writer in this sense of "work," and I do that with both teaching and writing. But he was not intellectually oriented in that way.

Sturgeon: He would be an example of someone who would not do what you're doing.

Dorn: Absolutely, and for reasons just as good as the ones I have for doing it.

Sturgeon: Could your reasons be related to the fact that you first encountered Olson in an academic situation, yet were able to have a close personal relationship with him?

Dorn: Very possibly. Frankly, I don't even remember my first intimate encounter with him in that sense. The fact is that when you talk about Olson with people who knew him you get a crazy-quilt impression and that is because certain people have very individual and intense and private effects on other people. They were all different. In my case, because I was an ignoramus from the Midwest and he was a sophisticate from the Northeast, he could do a lot for me. And you have to keep in mind, of course, that in those days and certainly at that place there was a situation—one that might be considered an embarrassing situation now—that would be described as the master-pupil relationship. It's not that he insisted upon that, it's just that that was the nature of it because he had that kind of power. I think it's a very effective learning experience. I mean it's not the same thing as education. It's different. It's educational. It didn't have many of the aspects of the conventional orthodox education. In other words, he didn't try to transmit the canon.

Sturgeon: He didn't?

Dorn: Not really. There were things he transmitted that were part of the canon. But it wasn't the canon. So the whole encouragement was, corny as it might now sound, to find out for yourself. And that's more easily said than done. So he tried to point out how you might go about it. That's why his education was always unconventional, and it's also why people handled it differently. For example, I chose to go from the viewpoint of the West. He was equally effective at pointing some people East. And I think that, like any good teacher, he found your inclination and temperament and intellectual capacity and tried to fashion a program for you—I hate that word *program* in the sense it's currently used—anyway, it worked.

Sturgeon: I'm not certain that the relationship you're describing excludes, if I can use the term in its current sense, "programs" in creative writing, where the master-pupil relationship is exactly what's cultivated. Yet you're saying that the relationship you had with Olson was quite different.

Dorn: I'm saying more than that. If there is a master-pupil relationship at such places at all, it's an institutionalized one, not an individual one. For example, one of the things the old guard at Black Mountain accused Olson of—and this was before he picked it up and took over—was a kind of Socratic relationship with his students, one that was very much resented.

Sturgeon: But you didn't resent it?

Dorn: No. But I didn't avail myself of their whole "program" either. I was aware that there was a problem—that it was much discussed. If Black Mountain was anything, it was self-aware.

Sturgeon: I'd like to ask you some questions about your present work. I'm particularly interested in what I consider to be a canyon opening out in the landscape of your writing since *Gunslinger*. Since then you've occupied yourself with a poetry of negative bulk, a negativity that expresses itself in frequently acid, occasionally fervent epigram. As you've made clear in several recent public statements, these writings aren't intended as poems in a conventionalized sense. Here's an example from *Hello, La Jolla*, "Sirius in January":

> It is swarming with planets
> Time definitely repeats itself
> That's its only job.

What range do you intend such a statement to have in the poetic field? How big is this poem?

Dorn: It's obviously not very big. It's a kind of notation, or, to use the current vocabulary, a kind of subscript on "the only thing that does not change is change itself," which gets back to Olson. But you don't have to know that, since it's basically obvious. People who pick up on its whole meaning would be people who acutely remembered that, who had their minds on the history of the transposition of such statements from that time.

Sturgeon: Here's another, from *Yellow Lola,* "The song of the vulgar boat-men."

> You will sink into the spiritual darkness
> of the animal kingdom
> And suffer infinite miseries of bondage,
> dumbness & torpor.

Are you preaching here, trying to get a message across, or are you concentrating more on the lyric aspect of what you've said? That is, if you don't mind explicating.

Dorn: I don't mind explication at all. But I should mention that *Yellow Lola* is a nonbook in a way, a king of dumping ground for *Hello La Jolla.* It's a bunch of scraps I didn't extract, scraps taken from my notebook by Tom Clark, who had a fascination with it.

Sturgeon: In other words, Tom Clark bears responsibility for this work?

Dorn: I take responsibility for it. For example, what you've just read is simply a bastardized farce of the Bible. But don't you think that that stuff's really obvious?

Sturgeon: Yes, exactly—that's why I'm interested in having you explicate it.

Dorn: Okay. Let me just say this about a thing like *Yellow Lola:* it gets its effect cumulatively. This is because of the extreme brevity of its components. Its effect can only come about from the entire roll of it. One thing might be interesting, sort of notable, but, psychologically, the book is cumulative.

Sturgeon: Taking that into consideration, then, explicate this one:

> "one must not be unkind"
> because it is demeaning
> to the person, but not because
> it is uninteresting practice.

Dorn: I'm making a statement that says that mere "positiveness," which would consist in, presumably, being kind, shouldn't be the explanation of why it's bad to be unkind. Because violence, cruelty, hurtfulness, and all the deeper psychological underpinnings of human nature are just as legitimate as anything else, although we must learn to restrict them.

Sturgeon: Some might say, because of the "acid" I've already mentioned with reference to your work, that you're doing just the opposite of restricting "violent underpinnings" in your writing. In other words, they might say that you proliferate them. How would you respond to that?

Dorn: I'd say they're stupid.

Sturgeon: Here's another one that seems related:

> One must not be guilty
> Of lowering the ideal
> by way of false claims of kindness

Why didn't you write that in sentence form? Why write it in lines?

Dorn: That's easy. Because writing it as if it were versified emphasizes its components and makes of it something that has to be considered slowly and digested, whereas a sentence is just something like running down a road. You don't notice every molecule in the white line.

Sturgeon: You want us to note these as perforations of form.

Dorn: Of course. In other words, this is another strike at utilizing falsehood. You see, I think the only unkindness is not to admit everything, which doesn't of course exclude the use I'm making here of compression.

Sturgeon: Yes. You're speaking of the manner in which you're presenting the language.

Dorn: Right. But I'm never presenting anything as language. I don't think poetry is language.

Sturgeon: What is it?

Dorn: I don't know what it is. I think that what language can do is no more than it ever does. The power of poetry is that by organizing what language can already do, language can do a little bit more. I don't think it has to do much more. That's why people who discuss the claims and expectations of language are extremely abhorrent. I mean everybody already knows about all that. We could be sitting in a bar or walking down the street and hear the most amazing thing. Nobody thinks it's a poem, but the fact is, it's just the same thing.

Sturgeon: To get back, then, to what you just mentioned as your "use of compression"—how would you compare your organization of language with that of, say, Tom Raworth? The little poem in *Levre de Poche,* for example:

> cold lives forever
> inactivity is cold
> therefore
> movement must cease

Dorn: Yes, that's from that little kangaroo pocket book that fits into his *Catacoutics.* David Southern did that book, and did a marvelous job. The poem's called "in Memoriam L. Wittgenstein." I consider it one of the most profoundly economic statements in modern philosophy. It's typical Tom Raworth—that bitterly intellectual twist in reality.

Sturgeon: Do you think there's any similarity between Raworth's work and your own?

Dorn: There may be some similarity, but not much. He's European and I'm not. That's the biggest difference. But he has a kind of love of compression that I certainly share. We always did, although in my earlier work it certainly doesn't look like it. Likewise, in his earlier work, there wasn't as much as there is now, but there was always more than with me. I think he's been a pretty good influence on my work as a whole—our association goes back to the sixties.

Sturgeon: Let's talk about something else now—I'd be interested to hear you discuss the primarily male orientation of your writing. Your "Statement for the Paterson Society," which you made back in 1960, is a good example of what I mean. In it you expressed very beautifully the delicacy and importance of the poet's relation to society, but you used what I would call a masculine tone: "Culture is based on what men remember, not what they do, fortunately. Even a civilized man who can read and write will occasionally exhibit this memory, at which times it is said of a man he acted with loveliness." This, it seems to me, involves a conscious choice in representing the gender of "the writer." In addition, your treatment of woman as a topic in writing seems to have received a peculiarly male emphasis. Stephen Fredman pointed this out to you in "Road-Testing the Language" in 1977, and you responded as follows: "I think there's only one Woman, anyway. It seems to me that men are multiple and women are singular . . . formally, all you need is one Woman. The presence of women always modifies circumstances a lot. They make it extremely social." Would you be willing to further analyze these past statements of yours?

Dorn: First of all, that Paterson statement is very sixties, fifties even, in that the rhetorical convention generally overruled such considerations. For me, women are much more universalized than men. For instance, in war, when it was fought, men fell "like sheaves of wheat." Men were harvested. Those things I said were uttered in accordance with a belief I hold, rightly or wrongly, that there's a basic difference between men and women. There is a certain kind of cultural cropping men undergo which I think differentiates them. These terms are so slippery, and very easily misunderstood, especially by those who would willfully misunderstand. If there's anything "sexist" in any of this it would be placing an undue honorific emphasis on women—which might be an extremely male thing to do. It's true that I feel very male. As far as literature is concerned, I think literature is superior to the writer. And as far as the so-called "women writers" are concerned, I value Fanny Burney a lot more than I do Alice Walker, the reasons being that she was a better writer and a better woman.

Sturgeon: What do you mean by "a better woman"?

Dorn: Better as an example of the experience of humankind. I mean that she had more access, that her intellection was greater, that her ability to assimilate and transmit experience was greater, that she's more interesting. Consideration of a female or a male writer's depiction of the female experience is a separate thing. For instance, I was just reading Michael Martone's James Dean story in *Alive and Dead in Indiana* in which he has taken on the role of a woman, and it was marvelous, I liked it and thought it was excellently done. I admire people who can do that. But my particular interest and talent doesn't do that. I think that people who can do it should do it, and people who can't, should stay away from it.

Sturgeon: Do you feel that you can't do that?

Dorn: I don't feel that I can't. No, I could do it, actually. But it's a strain I don't necessarily want to put on myself because I don't think that what I'd be able to say through it would be worth it.

Sturgeon: Do you think that what Haniel Long is saying through the voice of Malinche in *Malinche/Dona Marina* is worth it? That narrative seems to me to be powerfully feminine—I'm thinking particularly of her description of becoming Cortés's mistress.

Dorn: Well, Haniel Long was a very feminine guy, actually. That was probably the most important aspect of his intense Catholicism. One of the reasons I really have been attracted to his writings is because you don't get that in as pure a form from anybody else, man or woman. He's one of those minor, unknown, unread writers that can do more for you than anybody else. And of course his view of Malinche is extremely particular. There's been quite a bit of controversy and competition for the spirit of Malinche—the charge that she was the first traitor among the people and so forth.

Sturgeon: You're referring to Cordelia Candelaria's article "La Malinche, Feminist Prototype" [*Frontiers* 5, no. 2 (Summer 1980)].

Dorn: I am. Her essay deals with both sides of the question and is very fair and very valuable. There's also a woman, Margaret Shedd, who's written a novel about Malinche. But the point is that Malinche was probably the first negotiator in the hemisphere. In that sense she's extremely Greek, specifically a Sophist. Her vision is way beyond anyone surrounding her at the time. Cortés is seen in Long's book as the limitation and the brashness and the cruelty of the Western mind. And that's truth. The fact that some people are stupid enough to denigrate aspects of Long's style and ignore his other, totally powerful impetuosities, is just one of the faults of present prejudices and intellectual preemptions—and I don't have any time for that.

Sturgeon: You say the woman is standing for a civilization here, which really means that Long's not speaking through a female, but through a continent.

Dorn: Absolutely. Malinche is negotiating a terrible moment for Spain, as well as, obviously, other equally cruel civilizations, like the Aztecs and the Peruvians. You have to leave the Mayans out of that somehow, because they're different. But there's no question that she is the woman of the western hemisphere.

Sturgeon: You're getting back into that notion of "one woman."

Dorn: It's not my fault! If there had been a whole army of Malinches, things might have been different—I mean maybe they wouldn't have negotiated.

Sturgeon: Maybe not. Let's talk about another circumstantially "minor" writer, Robert McAlmon. You wrote the afterword to an unfinished poem of his, which was published by Dark Child Press in 1983 and posthumously titled *North America: Continent of Conjecture*. In it you say that McAlmon had a High Plains outlook in everything he said and a "hemispheric consciousness" behind everything he saw. So what drew you to Long seems to be ideologically similar to what drew you to McAlmon, a very different style of writer.

Dorn: McAlmon's is an absolutely true analysis here—removed, fairly frigid, very accurate, and therefore almost timeless. It's not necessarily going to endear itself to people of great prejudice, but it's certainly going to interest a lot of readers, particularly because it comes out of the blue of 1929, the year of the crash, and hasn't been seen since. And I think it's a reminder that his kind of writing, which is now to me the main mode at last, was being practiced, being ventured into, that long ago. Because while it's embedded in modernism, as McAlmon himself was, it's a departure from modernism.

Sturgeon: How so?

Dorn: Because rhetorically it's not obfuscating, which much of the modern was preoccupied with, in the obsessive desire to make all things psychological and to penetrate the interior. After all, that was the notion of the twentieth century, the hint that the interior was far greater than the exterior. This goes against the grain. I think McAlmon's poem is more interesting for us, living now, than it probably would have been had it had a wide circulation then, which it didn't.

Sturgeon: Our anxiety about the future seems to irritate you. Is this connected in some way to your admonition that "Yesterday which should have been one-half / our whole possibility is lost"?

Dorn: Sure. The courting of anxiety comes from a preoccupation with the future. There's no anxiety in the past—there are only lessons there. Knowledge of the past is the only thing that can reduce anxiety about the future. In fact, that's the nature of tragedy, that it's there to teach you about now. The future means nothing to me. The past is everything. The future flows into the past, and cultivates the past, and renews the topsoil—if that's possible.

From Imperial Chicago
Interview by Effie Mihopoulos

*A poet-in-residence program at Northeastern Illinois University
in Chicago hosted from 1970 to 1977 such influential poets as
Gwendolyn Brooks, Ted Berrigan, Tom Raworth, and Edward
Dorn. Chicago was an important outpost for Dorn's composing
books 2 and 3 of "Gunslinger." He saw Chicago as the West's
eastern port city. From there, he viewed the West in its entirety.
Chicago also brought the poet close to the cultural and political
vibe of the 1968 Democratic National Convention, a vibe whose
language was valuable source material for "Gunslinger."*

*In this interview with former student Effie Mihopoulos, Dorn
is at ease with the informality of the exchange. The nonchalant
intellect was a defining feature of many Beat writers, and
Dorn's cool included that, along with his hair-trigger impulse to
engage. Here the discussion ranges from Black Mountain gossip
to the influence of an anthropological perspective, from literacy
and how it is defined, to the poet in relation to "the market" and
a cynical salute to poetry's obsolescence.*

*The interview originally appeared in the December 1991 issue
of "LETTER eX," Chicago's poetry newsmagazine.*

Effie Mihopoulos: What was your whole experience at Black
Mountain like?

Edward Dorn: My life at the University of Illinois preceding that
had been pretty confused and not focused, so going to Black
Mountain didn't help the confusion much, but it certainly
made me focused. In fact, the confusion only increased. Black
Mountain was really good for confusing you. It was the dying
embers of a once-great educational experiment. There would
be lots of ways of characterizing it, but an intellectual adventure
was what it was for me, and I hadn't had one.

Mihopoulos: So it came at the right time in the development of your intellect?

Dorn: I was in my midtwenties. A bit late, but it wasn't going to happen earlier than that. I just learned about it because I didn't have those kind of connections to know about a place like Black Mountain. But when I think of Black Mountain, I don't just think of that experience, and not just the school, but also lots of other aspects of my life.

The summertime was really full of famous artists. Painters from New York. The winter was another kind of population. Those were the grim, hunkered-down, gritty regulars. It wasn't a happy place. Actually, it was wretched and miserable most of the time I was there, because it was just poor. That was a great lesson, but I have no idea what it taught.

Mihopoulos: It taught you to be who you are. How did Charles Olson influence you?

Dorn: Charles Olson gave me my whole impulse to be a writer and the fortitude to hold out. Intellectually, he was the most important person because he was like being around an expansionary force. He just made you get bigger somehow. It was really size, somehow, with him. He was huge himself, in terms of education and learning and the acquisition of information and knowledge of the world.

There were other people, too. The most important for me was Paul Laser. I took anthropology with him one year, and became an active amateur anthropologist from that year on. That very much obviously influenced the way I looked at the world. It was what I wouldn't have quite gotten with Olson, who was actually rather impatient with details a lot of the time. He tended to get grand and sweeping, and skip the details.

Mihopoulos: I didn't realize that you had studied anthropology, though with hindsight, it does show both in your writing and in your teaching, especially in the books that you recommended we read. There was always an "eye" there seeing things from a cultural anthropologist's viewpoint.

Dorn: I'm glad you noticed that because, aside from the literature I got there, I've had to go back and repair leaks in the plumbing, because at Black Mountain it wasn't a thorough education. It was a fanatical education. It covered a lot, but a lot didn't get covered. Nobody had heard of Milton there, for instance. You get out in the real world of literature, and you haven't read Milton, it's like a joke.

Mihopoulos: Though you're probably better off, not having read Milton.

Dorn: That was the point encouraged at Black Mountain, but I found that later to be quite untrue. Ignorance is not bliss.

But the other literature that was important to me there was anthropology. Things like Morgan's study of the Iroquois, in which he reveals, long before all the current people who are so aghast to learn it, that the Iroquois had instructed the framers of our Constitution a lot. Anyone who read a lot of anthropology in those days knew that. One of the things that I find irritating is that the people who have just woken up five minutes ago say, "See what they've been keeping from us all this time." It's so stupid. It's their own lazy habits of not reading that leads them into those problems. That's all been there all along.

Mihopoulos: Did you ever study anthropology with anyone else?

Dorn: No, just that one year with him was enough to set the foundation from which I knew how to read anthropology. I knew the basic books. Any education that has any quality at all is simply the foundation from which you then read the rest of your life.

My classmates that year (there were only about three of us) were Joel Oppenheimer and a guy who was a fabric designer later in New York, quite successfully. He was one of those graphic Black Mountain people; they were interesting, too. Only toward the end of Black Mountain did it seem to be dominated by writers. Just prior to that, in 1948, '49, '50 (I went there the first time in '50, then I went back again later, in '51), it was still under the influence of the painters and the architects who had been there. Buckminster Fuller had been there earlier. His influence was very detested by Olson, who thought he was the most awful, horrible goof who ever lived. Olson would have liked that joke which came later, "Buckminster Fuller's entire mind was formed in a toilet of a 747." But he has his great fans, too; everyone does.

From 1945 to 1950, that half decade, the influence was German refugees—intellectuals who found sanctuary at Black Mountain, which literally "took them in." You got only sanctuary, really. The salaries couldn't have amounted to much there. At the best of times, those people got like one hundred dollars a month. You got food, and the food was good, because there was a farm. You got isolation and sanctuary and Shangri-la, but no money. It was a very different kind of barter system and conception there. That you would do anything for anything other than money, is unthinkable now, because there doesn't seem to be anything other than money now. What would it be? Nobody's friends anymore, and food is dirt cheap. That's nothing anymore. Even the homeless eat, presumably. There's nothing left anymore other than that awful printing press money that we have, which is just like a disease.

Mihopoulos: How do world events, and their absurd surrealism, influence your poetry?

Dorn: I just write about it, report the events; I don't invent it. In that sense, the early anthropology certainly taught me how to be a witness. I take that as a big part of writing, being a witness.

Mihopoulos: So do you see the eye as the most important tool of the poet?

Dorn: Being a witness is your whole presence. The eye is obviously important. The human race is so exclusively optical that it's programmed to seek what's coming. We don't smell it or hear it much, so we really see it. But obviously the ear's important to me. I like to try not to mimic people at all, but to try to take their language and dress it up with a little richer vocabulary than they might have.

Mihopoulos: Do you think poetry is a dying art form in our society?

Dorn: Looking around and seeing what the connection in poetry is, it can be really disgusting and banal and not elevating and not ennobling and, in the end, except for an isolated clutch of a handful of people, unremunerative. So we're not even talking money with it, because except with the very obvious exceptions, all the attempts to get money out of it, are extremely demeaning, more demeaning than other things. A prostitute actually is the oldest profession, and it is legitimate, no matter what society thinks about it. You can name a lot of things like that, the most awful examples that you can come up with, and they have their own legitimacy. And poetry, in that respect, does *not*. It's free to the spirit, and there's no way to corrupt it. It will always be incorruptible. All you can do is corrupt yourself. Poetry itself is as unchangeable as the orbits. People write it more now, and writing has become one of the great human activities.

Mihopoulos: But it's essentially catharsis, because nobody reads it.

Dorn: Yes, but the whole readership of anything has been so inflated. There's the same number of readers relative to the population now who can read a poem without a lot of prompting and a lot of problems, as there always were. I don't think it's increased at all. Literacy has nothing to do with that.

Literacy today is a function that enables you to get around town: to locate addresses, to drive a car, and read the signs and not put the soap on the salad—all sorts of practical things that if you can't do, if you can't read, you can still get by, as we know people do. It's just more difficult, and they're always sort of living in fear if someone actually asks them what that says—because they know what to do with it, but just don't know what it says. They don't know how to read the word *walk*, but know when to walk, anyway. You can fake this stuff. Literacy is so low that you can even not possess it and still get by, and apparently a lot of people are doing that.

I think maybe there are 50,000 total readers of poetry in the country now and 10,000 of them might read John Ashbery and say, 3,500 of them might read Joe Blow in Montana and maybe 25 might read some guy who's living in the neighborhood. It all gets covered somehow. But that's all there are. In London, say, in John Keats's time, right after the turn of the century, Shelley's time and those people, there were maybe 5,000 readers of poetry. We know that from the sales figures. That can all be reconstructed. Books were quite expensive then, and not just anybody and their dog had a book. So that would be about the same number. That was considered an interest great enough to publish for, and it still is now. I don't think anything has changed in that sense.

Mihopoulos: You don't think the attitude has changed? In those days, there was an elite and other people were more illiterate, but writers were respected more. Whereas now, especially in American society (it's not as true, say, in Canadian society, or even in England), Americans are totally indifferent to writers except for blockbuster books by people like Judith Krantz.

Dorn: The *Collected Poetry of Jimmy Stewart* sold a lot.

Mihopoulos: Yes, and so did Rod McKuen, but can we call that poetry?

Dorn: The people who bought it called it poetry, obviously. But this is publishing by famous people. You get famous for something, and you can publish a book on anything. It could be poetry, or anything else. Like all the famous people who do their biographies. Somebody else does it. They're ghosted, or they're "as told to." And the "as told to" character might be ghosting it. These are contract jobs. The fact is, it doesn't matter what these books sell: poetry, biography, adventure, travel, my idea about this or Shirley MacLaine and how to go to Peru and get shook. It doesn't matter. It's what's selling. That's the book trade. I'm not willing to say that Jimmy Stewart can't write poetry. Anybody can write poetry. To me, they're absolutely disgusting, but they're no more disgusting than that guy who says he learned everything in life in kindergarten. That, in fact, is worse. Robert Ludlum, or something. He's the successor to Jonathan Seagull. That kind of writing has been around a long time. It's stuff that if it were squished in between your toes, you'd just jump and run to the shower and get it off.

There we get back to how we define literacy. If we want to widen the scope further and further till you finally do get out to the detergent with the lemon on it, then you've taken in everything. So if that's the definition of literacy, fine. Then all this stuff can be explained on that basis. If you're more exclusive . . . I don't think, by the way, that any true reader of poetry is an elitist. I know what you mean by that, but I think that the English reader of the first twenty years of the nineteenth century was a pretty serious character, and might have been quite a democrat, actually. There were, after all, followers of Coleridge in that group. Of course, there was also Lord Byron, who was having everybody on, and he was a great lord.

Mihopoulos: Well, it is a paradoxical kind of elitism, because there was a larger portion of the population at the time that didn't have the opportunity to become what those people were. In our society, if you're illiterate, in a sense, it's your own fault. You do have the opportunity to learn. Not always, because there are always certain environments in which it's harder. It's not the same growing up in the ghetto as growing up in the suburbs, where everything is at your disposal. But at that time, I think, there was much less of a choice than there is now. You're responsible, in essence, for your own literacy now.

Dorn: Let's just invent a term here. It's called "reverse elitism." I maintain anybody who can read a poem well and enjoy it and be informed by it, and actually exchange their own perceptual information with it (which I think is what reading's all about), may be part of the fortunate few, but I refuse to call that elitism, because elitism would be refusing to do that, in some way. It would be knowing how to do it, and not doing it.

There's a whole new class, and you'd only know this if you were in the academic racket, but there's a whole new class of people called "alliterates," people who can read but won't. And they're not doing me or Jimmy Stewart any good. They're all at Blockbuster Video.

Mihopoulos: Right. If your poetry was on a video, they'd listen to it or watch it then, but won't read it in a book. Do you think books are going to become obsolete?

Dorn: Books are obsolete right now, and have been for a long, long time.

Mihopoulos: So then it follows that poetry must be obsolete.

Dorn: It's obsolete, yeah. But so what? There are lots of great things that are obsolete. Kerosene lamps are obsolete, but there's no light like it in a cabin in northern Wisconsin. And maybe it's a good thing not to have electricity. Think of the best things in the world, actually, and they're all obsolete. Sure. But that's because a world that grows more and more venal and greedy and opportunistic makes things obsolete at a great rate. And what they replace it with is something pretty awful and foul and cheap and temporary and terrible. So poetry is real obsolete.

Mihopoulos: Well, that's what I meant by dying art form. So how does it make you feel to be working in an obsolete art form?

Dorn: It makes me feel great. It makes me feel like I'm working with something that's good enough to be obsolete. I'll tell you, horses are obsolete, and horses are great. A 1932 Packard Phaeton is obsolete, one of the greatest cars ever made. Need I go on about obsolete?

The giveaway, actually, was this. I grew up with this; I was fifteen years old in 1945, real postwar, the curtain came up, and life began. At that time, there was this word that came on as one of the most smart, zippy ideas ever uttered. It came from Detroit, from automobile engineers. It was called *obsolescence*. It was going to save everybody. It meant that if you had the engineering right, this car door, after ten thousand openings and shuttings, would fall off and be sent to the junkyard. It would keep people employed.

The 1991 version of that is recycling. You don't even wait till it falls off: you just pour everything out of it and recycle it immediately. And that becomes a polluting industry in itself. Because nobody wants to live downwind from a polyurethane recycling plant. Like those diet pop jugs that people throw back in. Nobody wants to live downwind from that.

Mihopoulos: Years ago, you taught a class at Northeastern Illinois University called Classical Greek Mythology and the American West. It blew everybody's mind, especially at the time, that you could even think of connecting these two things. The fact that you did it successfully totally mystified everyone. How did that relate to your writing, since you were working on *Gunslinger* at the time?

Dorn: I was in the middle of writing *Slinger* in those years. In fact, I did a lot of book 2 in Chicago. It was just that whole preoccupation with Homeric and Virgilian characters, and more so Virgil because *The Aeneid* is really post-Homer going West. It's really just soul-searching, sojourning, and meeting phenomena and populations. What's going on. There's usually nothing going on, and everything going on. It's that kind of thing, like raw, human, ordinary life. Dressed up in sort of legendary, fantastic figures. And that's what I was talking about. But you know, the whole Western question, after Black Mountain and Laser and Olson, that was my preoccupation with the subject, and it still is. People who set out to write for the long haul don't see the mountains behind the forest. They don't start looking behind each thing that they're doing.

Mihopoulos: They only see the craft, and nothing else, like the Iowa people sometimes.

Dorn: I like craft. But when you only concentrate on craft like that, it's hideous, like link sausages.

Mihopoulos: Does the place you're living in influence your writing? You were already working on *Slinger*, set in the West, when you were living in Chicago, this very urban environment.

Dorn: Chicago is the capital of the West. There's a whole book that is based on the premise that Chicago was the colonial exploiter of the Great Plains, in the same way that London controlled Kenya or India, in that same sense. It loaned the money, it bought the crops, it laid down the law. It's fascinating. Chicago is an imperialist place, in that sense. The Great Plains has an area and a gross national product and a transaction far larger than many countries for that relationship. At one time, I'm sure, it was more true than it is now. So it's part of the West. You know, people call it the Midwest, but really the West is the West.

Mihopoulos: Do you think about long poems like *Gunslinger* as narrative poems?

Dorn: Sure. Maybe that's a bit gratuitous, I suppose. It tells a story. It's not much of a story; it's a thinnish excuse. The bare bones of the thing. It's the simplest thing, just taking a trip. Just on the road. Like *On the Road* didn't invent on the road. Everything was on the road. That's what the Greek epics are, on the road. *The Iliad* is fixed; that's the difference. But *The Aeneid* and *The Odyssey* are on the road. *Slinger* is just on the road in more modern times, with horses and stagecoaches and fake technology.

Mihopoulos: While *Gunslinger* is a long narrative poem, it's very concise. Do you think of it as a long poem, a narrative poem, or both?

Dorn: The period of its composition was really stretched out. It was really a portable poem. I could write it in Chicago, San Francisco, Kansas, England because it started off with the kind of distance I got on the subject and my feelings for the West. All the times I had been transported back and forth across it, was one big vision.

Gunslinger's narrative is essentially linguistic, because it starts out with a series of standard settings, in cowboy times, with a coach in Billy the Kid country and it's on the border. It goes through all those kinds of references. This is the excuse for using a kind of Spanglish: not exactly, but a kind of Chinook jargon Spanish which runs all the way through it. Because it is the Southwest, but that's in there for flavor, and to zip it once in a while. And it's just a series that moves along. Somebody looks out the window and says something like, "Hey, man, it's a crazy landscape." Then the talk goes on from there about what's actually in it. Then I collect strange words like the word *hoodoo*, which I thought was some kind of magic or religious thing. It turns out to be, not spelled quite that way, a geological term for certain kind of moundy-like things. So that gets conflated with a certain drift of the conversation which might be about magic or perceptions.

That becomes increasingly the poem's preoccupation. How do puns and ambiguities of language enter into everyday life? Because this poem is like everyday life back then: it's a time trip.

These people are taking a stagecoach. I've tried to make it more exotic by having six driverless horses. At first, I thought, "Wow, six driverless horses, fantastic! That's amazing. Boy, what am I going to do with that?" Well, I did nothing with that. Because by the time it came around again and it was time to do something with it, I thought, "Well, I'm not going to go back and do it. So they're driverless, to hell with it. That doesn't mean anything. There's just no driver." In other words, the whole idea is just generating this in the reader also.

We're like dogs to a certain extent. We go around and sniff here and there, and we may not go back. The circle may never be completed. That's why I said, "All right, if that's what's happening, then that's what's happening." Driverless horses because really I don't want to have to bother with having to deal with a driver. I don't want to describe him. I just want to stay inside the coach. So these horses know where they're going: The horse knows the way to carry the sleigh, through the something and the drifting snow. Maybe it comes from that kind of stuff: over the river and through the woods, to Grandmother's house we go. It's the same thing. He didn't have a driver, either. The horse knows the way. That's what horses do.

Mihopoulos: It's archetypal.

Dorn: They're known for their intelligence in mythology, although anybody who's been around horses knows that they're dumb as shit. They don't even have an intelligence, what they've got is an incredibly active and really dangerous and vibrating nervous system. They're all nerves. In so far as maybe their brains are extensions of their nervous systems, then the nervous system *is* their intelligence, except draft horses. I grew up with draft horses. They're really placid. They weigh about 1,500–2,000 pounds, like a ton. The only thing is, you don't want to have your foot underneath when they take a step to the side and shift weight, because you're talking big.

Mihopoulos: Political poetry can often veer into diatribes or dated nonsense. It was interesting in your comments during your reading at Northeastern that you said about selecting the poems for *Abhorrences* that you had to throw out a lot of them, because "It was just trash." How do you distinguish between writing poetry that's true, but still has a political message, and political vehemence?

Dorn: I think, in the case of *Abhorrences,* the standard there was rather overwrought and a little too vicious and a little like really getting a knife in. But then you could look at this and say, "But actually, the knife's into what? when it comes right down to it?" You're not separated enough from it. So I tended to choose the things that got off a little bit, lowered the temperature on things, got a little bit cold, a little high-minded, a little superior, not too involved. A lot of stuff was spinning around a kind of pointlessness, or it's a rant pure and simple.

One of the things about political poetry is that you have to sort of imply to the reader that this is a rather intimate situation in which I'm going to say something that's rather stiff to you, and you're going to like it, because actually you agree when it comes right down to it. You have to feel how to do that in a poem. It's presumption, but it's with the kind of presumption that you can't offend the reader or alienate the reader into saying, "Wow, that *is* a presumption." You have to include the reader.

Mihopoulos: Do you view your poetry as political poetry?

Dorn: Absolutely. It's my way of voting early and often.

A Correction of the Public Mind

Interview by Kevin Bezner, 1992

"American Poetry Review" remains one of the best-distributed po-etry publications in the country. None of Edward Dorn's poems was published in "American Poetry Review" while he was alive. But the magazine published Kevin Bezner's interview with Dorn in the September–October 1992 issue, preceding the presidential election.

In Radio Ezra Pound style, Dorn hurled a few philippics at ravenous consumers and power-hungry politicians. When he refers to "Abhorrences" as "a correction of the public mind," he affirms the Augustan nature of his satire. At the root of his scorn is concern. A rationalist ethos underlies his work. At a lec-ture he gave not long before this interview, Dorn told a class of graduate students: "The Poet needs a moral force. Morality will give the poem authority. To embody that Voice, the poet must be more, and have moral integrity."

Kevin Bezner: One of the things that's striking about *Abhorrences* is that there are over 140 poems. It's basically a decade's worth of work, and it's like a daybook, or a diary, in a sense. Did you have the idea of a sequence from the start?

Edward Dorn: It was preconceived. It didn't take any particular brilliance to see that it was going to be an abhorrent decade. That was pretty clear right off. The word *abhorrence* occurred to me right off, but then I came up with the plural, a made-up word. I call it chronicle because it's dated, for the most part. I saw that it was going to make its own form, and I was just going to let it be what occurred to me. Obviously, it had to be way over-written to get the book. That's about a third of what was done.

Bezner: You were looking for the right feel?

Dorn: If you're paying attention to vulgarizations, you're going to have way more material than you need. It's quite possible that some of the things I didn't include or couldn't make up my mind about are as interesting as anything in the book. The only thing I did in a formal way in terms of the chronology is date everything. If you look at the dates, they come in batches because there are spots when the news is particularly abhorrent. It's like what journalists call a hot news day or a slow news day. Tom Clark was here in Boulder when these things started out and we shared a lot of abhorrences. A lot of it came out of our association and talking about the possible solutions to the overriding solipsism that afflicts modern poetry.

Bezner: You mean poems that focus solely on the self without the external?

Dorn: Right, and how it might be effective to shed as much of the self as possible and let the actual state of affairs do more of the work; in a way, reducing the interference of the poet.

Bezner: So many of these poems are short, even though there are long poems in the book, and they seem to be those concise moments that you pick. There's a stripped-down quality about the book.

Dorn: A correction of the public mind, which is endlessly correctable in my view, tends toward the axiomatic. Of course, you have to watch that too. You don't want to let that become the main thing. You can't reduce everything to a maxim. Another thing, one of the overriding attitudes and pervasive methods was to take as much exception as possible. There's no one place you can go and say this is the problem. Whether this is true or not, and it's arguable, it's good for the method. You have to have a similarity of concentration over an extremely long period of time, and you have to trust that it's correct.

Bezner: Did you worry at all that by focusing on current things that it was a risk in the sense that down the road people might not be interested in this, or find it too political?

Dorn: I never worried about it being too political because that's the one thing that is sorely missing from American poetics. About whether people would be interested in it or not, I suppose that's always a risk. Are people going to be interested in your feelings? That's less likely.

The risk I thought was, "Well, I'm going to be doing something for ten years and I'm not going to be publishing much." In the game I'm in, if you don't publish, people think you're not doing anything. On the other hand, a decade is a form. Who knows whether they're going to live a decade?

One of the basic propositions of *Abhorrences* is that the only poetry that really matters and the only poetry that anybody might want to pay attention to is the poetry that exhibits a certain kind of aggression towards the readers. I don't see any reason to write any other kind of poetry at this moment and by this moment, I mean from now to whatever happens at the end of the second millennium. It's not that far off.

Given where we're at, nobody is going to be aesthetically enlightening, certainly not if you look back over the last 150 years.

Bezner: Give me an example of somebody aesthetically enlightening.

Dorn: There isn't going to be a Shelley between now and the year 2000.

Bezner: Because of society?

Dorn: No, because that's not available as a poetic problem or endeavor. A recommencement of what poetry means would have to occur before that's possible. Poets are now like some straggling band. It's a cleanup operation. It's mopping up, really. That's all right. Any period has its job to do. People who are writing poems from their experience or trying to advocate what people should think, all of that is useless. They're just taking up room on the scene.

Bezner: Lawrence Ferlinghetti once complained of how there are no gadflies in contemporary poetry. You seem to be making the same complaint, and you seem to be becoming even more of a gadfly than you've ever been.

Dorn: Ferlinghetti is a gadfly in his best work, the Nixon poems. I agree with that. That's not exactly my view. Actually, I'm not very political. I probably have more sympathy to the Left, but the Left is pretty ridiculous most of the time. There is no satisfaction in any of these positions. My interest in politics derives from how it reveals human hypocrisy and self-interest.

Bezner: One of the best poems for me is "I'm clean, how about you," which basically says we're all corrupt and what are we going to do about it? Also, "Self Criticism," which is spoken in the voice of the contemporary American who's completely hypocritical.

Dorn: In "Self Criticism," I was trying to put myself, not very seriously by the way, in the position of an American person who would be like a Chinese person on the rack, or even a subject of the Inquisition, or a victim of Stalinism, or any number of totalitarian states. All of those things have been an attempt to do the one thing that everybody knows you can't do, which is actually, from the outside, get inside the mind and make it conform. To me, what's being sought is total control. Looking in the face of the overwhelming propensity for cruelty on the part of the state, there's no other way to think. You know it wants total control. It's the beast. There's no doubt about it. It's the beast.

Bezner: In "HomoSap" you compare Reagan to Faust. What you're talking about is that Faust sold one soul, and Reagan sold or wanted to sell more souls.

Dorn: All of them. But then, he was the greatest hireling of the dark powers that we've known. Also in there is a certain hesitancy to put Nixon on a level with Reagan. Nixon was human. He was a beast, but he was human. For instance, his proposal, quite naive in a sense: "The trouble with the poor is that they don't have any money. Let's give them some." That's a brilliant thought. It seems obvious, but for a politician of that rank to have actually said that is pretty amazing. Whereas Reagan said the opposite: "The poor need money. Let's take it away from them." There's a vast difference in that.

Again, one of the preoccupations of this book is in discriminations. If you don't discriminate, you can't condemn, because condemnation without discrimination is just another mindless exercise. The more people who don't know, the easier it is to feed their channels. You can get them to behave as you want them to, which in this particular society really boils down to consumption, and that's about it.

Bezner: Excess, consumerism, materialism?

Dorn: Oh, sure. It's a very simple program and it's very stupid, of course. But it only works in the short run, and it validates the free market and legitimizes growth.

Bezner: What this poetry does is make you wake up to the hypocrisy that is out there, but also in your own life. I'm sure you hoped this would happen.

Dorn: It's not as if you're doing anything important by writing a book of poetry these days. But a poet can't think that. You do it anyway. The greed of poetry is just as reprehensible as anything else, because you'd use the last tree to write it.

Bezner: The eighties were particularly abhorrent. What creates a decade like this?

Dorn: To understand the eighties you have to understand the seventies. That's the decade everyone pretends didn't exist. It was introduced by Nixon in the greatest psychological upheaval, Watergate—the gate with no water—the interregnum under Ford, which was one of the most placid and pleasant episodes in American history; then Carter, who is actually all right. But because he initiates things Americans have their minds set against, this led to a reaction. Ronald Reagan was perfect for that. The sad thing about this country is that when the majority exercises if power, it's reactionary. In a way, the majority deserves these stupid little minorities that have selfish little programs, one-issue enclaves of people who don't have any vision, their one focus of opposition is toward this majority—because the only time the majority gets together is under a Reagan. It wants to say, "If you've got a dictator who's on our side, let him torture all he wants. Let him create poverty. Give him free rein." That's finally the message. That's about the only thing the majority in this country can think to do. So it earns its bad reputation. It doesn't take much imagination to see that it could actually do something else. It could have followed Carter's lead. It chose not to.

I don't think that the eighties were particularly abhorrent. They were specifically abhorrent. It was so abhorrent that its velocity is still with us. The eighties, in a way, will never end. Everybody talks about the nineties, how they're cutting their hair differently and so forth, but it's still the eighties under a different brand name and we've got a Bush who insists that everybody doesn't speak in complete sentences. Sometimes he's funny in a bitter, bitter way. He's replaced one set of goons with another set of goons. That was the style set up by Nixon. He imported the California goons and they were a particularly obnoxious lot. Let's not repeat their names. They were really crude, primitive. By the time you get to the second generation of California goons with Reagan, we get cookie cutouts. Meese was a cookie cutout. But they're vicious, desperate, criminal cookie cutouts. Oh, terrible people. So with Bush, it's Texas's turn. In one sense, this book is a history of my own thoughts about things. At the same time, it's a history of the actual changes. I don't think that there's anything in *Abhorrences* that couldn't be verified by observation. It's quite empirical. In that sense, it's scientific. I don't think the thinking in this book is peculiar to me. The statemental quality is obviously peculiar to me, the way I tend to project and couch things. I also like to think that this is a national book. I don't think it's regional.

Bezner: You also get into personal abhorrences. The new versions of Olson's *Maximus Poems* and *Collected Poems* published by California, which are big and unwieldy, the treatment of Richard Brautigan.

Dorn: Olson was trashed by the West Coast and Brautigan by the East Coast in similar ways. There's a certain kind of coercion between the coasts in everything but the literary. In literary affairs, that's where the antagonism still exists. They have a low tolerance for one another. Brautigan never got a good review in New York. He was considered simple-minded. The idea that Olson could be taken up by the West Coast, that's a more perverse case. They don't understand his universalization of mind, which is scholarly, intellectual, and which California has always mistrusted. They're Buddhists, right? They're Hindus. All the things he was not. He respects history and his forebears and the genetic lineage that is anathema to Californians. They can't pay attention to that. It is the new polyglot nation of the United States. California is a nation. In their recent effort to get the French pill, which of course isn't going to happen because of the antiabortion lobby, they even say, "Look, they can't keep us from having it because we're as big as France." They don't mean just in size, they mean culturally. It's banned, but they're going to have it anyway because it represents the libertarianism they think they must have in order to exist. In other words, the California attitude is "There's nothing we can't have." In fact, it's true, because there's a lot that they shouldn't have that they've got, and it's killing them.

Bezner: One of the things that Olson does so well is capture the essence of American culture. That is what *Abhorrences* and *Gunslinger* have done. Is that something you think you distinctly owe Olson, who was your teacher?

Dorn: He definitely taught me how the boundaries of what could be included in a poem could be breached. No question of that. I wouldn't have had any idea of that if I hadn't studied with him. Characteristically, we're quite different. He was a Catholic, I am a Protestant. I am from the Midwest, which means I'm cynical, deeply cynical. He was not. He was deep down a Catholic, so his respect for authority is much greater than mine. Those differences were basic by nature. Being a Midwesterner, I would see the unbelievably romantic and poetic values of his work, which has been slighted by people who write about it, who are much more interested in and taken by and are anxious to promote the scholarly and intellectual sources that are there. But his way of casting language and making history vibrant is extremely poetic.

Bezner: Just the way lines fall on the page. It seems you have that, too.

Dorn: It's wonderful to share that with him. I learned a lot of that from him. But I never really could feel the faith in practicing what he thought of as breath. My line is never so radically long or short as his is, which is where the crucial point comes, the faith you have in the throw back from the end, and how the phrase is going to pick up again. I always mediated that. In that sense, I'm more conservative than he is. In fact, we really had our disagreements. The thing about Olson and myself is that we were never really friends.

Bezner: I would have thought you were friends, with that effort he took in setting up *A Bibliography on America for Ed Dorn*.

Dorn: I was always his student.

Bezner: But you must have been an extraordinarily special student to him.

Dorn: I was a special student. We were close in the sense that our interests and our sense of morality and integrity were rather aligned. Our loyalty to one another and our allegiance was not based so much on friendship as on a concern for poetry and intellection and knowledge and public morality, which, in fact, I found him flawless on. He had much better friends, people who were close in that sense, but then a lot of people were not as close as we were in this other sense.

After Black Mountain, I had to educate myself. The education there was about procedure and methodology. I did get my whole interest in the West organized there. Of course, I went there with it. I don't regret the *Bibliography*. That was the course I took. It was my graduate studies, really. Black Mountain was just what you made of it. It wasn't undergraduate, graduate, or anything else. It was individualized. You expressed your interests, and were allowed to carry them as far as you wanted. I studied a year and a half with Olson. That finished me off. That was it.

Then I left. I became an itinerant worker, always reading. But I was writing, corresponding with him. Actually, it was a movable school in that sense. Black Mountain didn't die so much as it dispersed.

Bezner: It's amazing who was there. John Cage, Josef Albers, yourself, Olson, Creeley.

Dorn: From the end of the war until it folded, particularly, because before that it was an experimental school as it was then understood, but still rather conventional. After all, despite his critique on the study of the classics, John Rice [dean of Black Mountain] was a classicist. The emigré population fleeing Germany gave it the kind of faculty you couldn't ever afford unless you set yourself up as a sanctuary. That was a matter of historical luck. Because I was pretty uneducated and still am in a way, I couldn't have anticipated the people I'd be in contact with. Of course, Olson appreciated that, too. Although he was a powerful force and really full of strong prejudice about lots of things, his admiration for intellection was never in doubt. That's what the school represented. It was an intellectual academy. One of the things people say now is "I wish there was a Black Mountain around," without realizing that it was only around then and never reproducible because it was the result of a certain configuration of people who coincided at that time. It wasn't by design.

Statements on Olson, Bunting, and Duncan

Edward Dorn was a poet and writer, not a scholar or critic of the work of Charles Olson, Basil Bunting, or Robert Duncan. His comments on their work were often sought by academic conference organizers and literary researchers because of his personal contact with them and his ability of articulate how that contact affected his own thinking.

His relation to Olson is complex, even as he tries to clarify it by identifying himself as Olson's student rather than a student of Olson. Dorn recognized Bunting, with whom he had a couple of chance encounters, as one of Charles Olson's World War II generation, a friend of Pound, an elder statesman, an intelligent operative, but also one known to fall asleep during poetry readings at Morden Tower in Newcastle, England. Dorn's relation to Duncan was less complex because they were more distant. Dorn did not study under Duncan at Black Mountain, but his wife Jennifer did at Kent State in the fall of 1972, when Dorn and Duncan briefly taught in the same English department.

Dorn's statement at the University of Iowa's Olson Conference in November 1978 was edited by Sherman Paul for a videotaped record of the proceedings. Paul's abbreviated version of Dorn's remarks is the only record. Dorn's contribution to the panel discussion on the Poetries of California at the Modern Language Association Meeting at the University of California at San Diego in 1994 are from notes that Dorn intended to expand and complete, but declining health prevented. The brief interview on Basil Bunting is verbatim, "just as it comes out of the can," Tom Pickard's 16mm film about Basil Bunting produced for the BBC.

From the Charles Olson Conference at University of Iowa

November 1, 1978

ı just picked up John Fowles's new novel, *Daniel Martin,* and found this quote from Antonio Gramsci's *Prison Notebooks:*

"The crisis consists in the fact that the old is dying and the new cannot be born. In this interregnum, a great variety of morbid symptoms appear."

I thought I would speak in terms of being Olson's student rather than a student of Olson. In that respect I'd like to simply trace what I am as his product.

I've always thought he was a great teacher. That was my experience of him. It occurred to me lately that perhaps one of the marks of a teacher is what he or she might not actually provide you with, because I've seen what he left out for me.

The whole question of the West was of course a public gift, and meant to be as such. A lot of people have shared in that, and I never, even from the first, considered it personal to me necessarily, or ever to have priority over it.

One of the things Olson stressed to me a great many times was that we were living in a world that wasn't really happening in any great sense. He spoke of it as an interim very often, and I always took that to mean one could clearly get on with the work without that much public interference, or in fact private interference. It's not that unique an idea, but in the early fifties, like a lot of things, I hadn't really thought of it that way and I hadn't really heard that.

I'll give a short account of some of the things which most influenced me from Olson's thinking; for instance, the fact that he valued the book as a form, without actually qualifying what the book might be, whether it were poetry or long essay, in other words, regardless of the subject matter. He used to say, "It's good to write a book" as such. Therefore when I came to writing *Gunslinger,* I thought naturally and immediately of writing them as books, not necessarily in the Greek sense at all, but just from a sense of the fifties. A book is that kind of instrument. I still think of writing as being something expressed in books.

This book is called *The Z-D Generation.* It's by Ed Sanders. It's recent. For any of you who know his investigative poetry statements, indeed it incorporates a lot of statements that go back to the very beginning of his campaign to alert America, back to say 1961 when he was carrying his statements around in his backpack in the Lower Eastside. If I were to just read this out loud, you wouldn't know what Z-D meant necessarily, unless you were very good at crossword puzzles perhaps. I'll just tell you right out that they are Émile Zola and Denis Diderot.

> A New Generation
> We propose the creation of
> The Z—D Generation.
> Z—D!　　　Z—D!　　　Z—D!
> 　　ZOLA-DIDEROTS!
> Émile Zola, Denis Diderot
> both concerned
>
> with the PRECISE, IMMEDIATE
> Application of DATA
> Of Historical Reality, of Encyclopedic Wisdom
>
> 　　in its own time
> 　　AS IT HAPPENS,
>
> In correcting
> the drift of a particular civilization.

I was happy to bring this along because what I'm really doing with this is covering so far what I've been able to discover about the eighteenth century, which is precisely what Olson didn't give me. In fact, I've suspected recently that he so much didn't give it to me that he meant for me to get it. Zola and Diderot cover a part of the eighteenth century that in fact I'm not. My interest, to trace it, comes through Ezra Pound's sources, through the kind of material he was making available; e.g., W. E. Woodward. Going through Woodward's bibliographies I discovered a book by Edgar Bauer, a very elegant book from about 1925, *Jefferson and Hamilton*. It's a history of the last quarter of the eighteenth century from the standpoint of what the journalism was like; for instance, one learns about how great a journalist Philip Freneau was. It became quite evident to me that, even though I'd always been aware that he's called the first American poet, I couldn't quite see from reading his verse that

that meant anything more than that. But his life as a journalist looks brilliant. To a certain extent he was the gramaphone of Jefferson, who being the first really masterful politician in this country, knew how to hide behind his agents. It was largely with Freneau that Jefferson fended off the then right-wing. I don't know whether they were right-wing nuts of the variety we have now or not.

My own feeling now is that part of the reason I'm interested in the eighteenth century almost exclusively is because it's an outrageous present position to take. That's one reason. The other reason is that, in the literary sense, I find it a great taste to my mind. I also promote endlessly the prose of Johnson in say *The Lives of the Poets* as being my sense of how to correct the drift.

On Bunting with Tom Pickard, 1994

Tom Pickard: Ed, when did you first become acquainted with Bunting's work?

Edward Dorn: I first heard of Basil Bunting when I went to Black Mountain College, which was a small, extremely radical, experimental college in North Carolina which flourished from about 1933 to around 1958. I went there to study with Charles Olson who was a follower and believer in Ezra Pound and he mentioned Basil Bunting along with Zukofsky and people like that and I heard their names for the first time. I had not read their work and I wasn't, in fact, to read their work until years later. At that time I never dreamed that I would ever meet Basil, but do remember the stories of this sort of adventurous sailor-poet who would appear in a port in Texas and disappear. His reputation, or his legend in America began as part of the reference system surrounding Ezra Pound, for me, and I assumed for everybody else. Having known Basil's work later, and having come to realize its relationship with music and painting and its sense of structure and its care for structure, I think probably it's significant that there were musicians and painters at Black Mountain that he would have known about or respected.

Pickard: How do you see the difference between Pound's and Bunting's approach or understanding of power?

Dorn: Well one of Ezra Pound's problems—he had a lot of problems with the public—was that his energy was seemingly boundless, no matter what he was doing. Ezra Pound said he played tennis like an insane kangaroo. It was a little bit like that politically as well. I mean his hunger and obsession with order is how I see his slip into fascism and for that he's much criticized. You know, fascism means a lot of things to a lot of people. I mean for instance now is it fascism when somebody says if you don't have democracy I'll kill you? Which seems to be American foreign policy. I don't know, I mean some people would say that's fascism, but we know what we're talking about when we talk about Pound. I think he was crazy by some definition about those things. It looks more and more like his economic system is not as crazy as it appeared.

I think Basil, actually, his experience with power was grounded in his life. He had been a foreign agent of one description or another, he had diplomatic experience, he was an expert in communications. He rubbed elbows with people who actually were in power, but Pound was never close to any of that—so that with Pound it was all theoretical and therefore mental really. But with Basil Bunting he actually worked as a government agent of one kind or another—so when he spoke of power and authority and its uses and its misuses he was speaking from the standpoint of having actually observed it. Pound never did that. Pound could write a book like *Jefferson and/or Mussolini* because he was so far from it that he could put those two names together. Nobody who knew anything in the practical sense would have done that, they would have been much more discriminating. But of course by doing that Pound was trying to be outrageous. One can't forget that, because part of his whole system of propaganda was to be shocking. He was an early bad boy, for sure. But it's always possible to underestimate. I mean one shouldn't call Ezra Pound crazy because in fact he was not strictly speaking crazy. He valued Basil Bunting for the reasons that made Basil a practical politician in that sense. He knew he knew about the Middle East. In fact he referred to Basil as his "correspondent in the Middle East." I mean he depended on Basil to transmit that culture to him, which he didn't have. The mark of any great man or woman is that they know what they don't know. People who are not great don't know that, I think.

Pickard: Ed, why do you think Bunting was neglected?

Dorn: Well there's this peculiar interregnum, a vacuum in his career which is more notable than almost anybody you can think of. He was more than neglected, he was ignored, or perhaps even, shut out in a strange way. He didn't have a self-promotion apparatus, which most people who become famous in something so worthless as poetry have to have and have to attend it pretty much every day. That would be a question that would be aside.

When somebody is an adventurer and a poet, or a diplomat and a poet, or who has had other experiences than something that emerges from the academy he [would be] generally resented and an object of suspicion. You know it's true that there are academic poets, but most poets have had some connection, whether academic or not—it doesn't make any difference—they've come out of the academy somehow. I mean somebody in the academy has noticed and promoted them, or championed them and so forth. This has been the mark of the twentieth century. T. S. Eliot wasn't an academic, but he was the ultimate academic, to the academy. He worked in a bank, he worked as a publisher, an editor, in all sorts of things, but [the] care and protection coming from the academy made him the greatest academic of all. Basil had no protectors, no champions, no one to look after him in the halls of power. It seems ridiculous to speak of the halls of power of poetry, but in those places where one's name is nurtured and generated and increased. And then, he was discovered by travelers, rediscovered by travelers, some of them American, some English, people who made their way to Newcastle, largely at the invitation of Tom Pickard. That's what resurrected him. It was the people who were interested purely in poetry, not in reputation.

Pickard: Do you think anyone else played a role in Bunting's neglect?

Dorn: Well Eliot occupied the position of power and one of his strategies was to write essays and redefine what literature could be and was according to his own lights. Basil wouldn't have been a threat exactly. I mean what could threaten T. S. Eliot? But he certainly wouldn't have conformed to what Eliot wanted, as a buttressing element in his own position in the canon. We have to remember that in those days the canon hadn't even been questioned. It was assumed there was a canon and the canon was all right. Eliot was maniacal in the protection of his career. There's something very, very strange that I've never quite been able to figure out, but he had this strange prescience about his own career in the sense that somehow he managed to hit a mark down the way so far off that it's astonishing. His papers are going to be opened either the year after or the year before the Kennedy assassination papers which is going to be in 2027 or 2028. That's just amazing that he could, in a postmortem sense, opportunistically take advantage of such a mark on the board of time. This is unheard of, it's unprecedented. It's quite amazing. Maybe he killed Kennedy, I don't know. [Laughs]

But quite seriously, when one wants to talk about fascism, I had a lot of trouble with this business of Ezra Pound's fascism. No real fascist would want Ezra Pound around as a fascist. It's like his tennis-playing style—he would be like a kangaroo fascist in the midst of fascists. I mean he would draw a lot of attention. So that never really makes much sense, whereas Eliot was quite a serious and subversive and stealthy fascist. It's not just the phrases in *The Waste Land* that have been making people blink when they skim over them, but the whole deportment of his life was power-mad and authority-oriented. For an American to join the Church of England has to be like some kind of attempt at power I suppose, spiritual power. It's interesting why he couldn't quite go to Rome, so he went to the last place Rome stopped off before it was stopped. We could talk about the effect of that on these islands. T. S. Eliot was the midwife who was constantly trying to kill the baby. He was the abortionist of the postmodern movement, he controlled who was going to be born and who wasn't, insofar as he could.

Pickard: How did you first meet Basil?

Dorn: I came to England in the autumn of 1965 as a Fulbright lecturer at the University of Essex and was invited to give a reading at the Morden Tower in Newcastle in February 1966. I met him over lunch when he was working on the the financial pages of the *Newcastle Journal*. He was a copy editor or proofreader and I somehow got the idea that his incredibly thick glasses had come from his straining his eyes over those pages. So we had lunch and that was my first exposure to his immense conviviality and amiability, and sweetness, really. I had never seen that in the same person— a first-rate intellectual—because I was always used to intellectuals being quite mean and difficult and awful. So that was quite a shock. To see someone who obviously had a first-rate mind *and* was a nice person, was really a brand-new experience for me.

So over the years, along with many other travelers, went back to Newcastle, to the Morden Tower reading series which, as far as I could tell, in my judgment, was the most exciting and possibly the most important place to read in England in those days. Certainly it had the most continuous series of poets that I was interested in and felt part of than, say, any other place in England, and I met people there who I wouldn't have met otherwise. But the constant reference for me and desire to go there was to hang out with Basil Bunting. The Morden Tower was like a legionnaires' tackle room in the wall. It was via this pub, the Northumberland Arms. I remember one instance of reading at the Tower and Basil came in all smiles and his usual gracious self and I started to read. He sat down in a chair and smiled, he had a great smile, and promptly fell asleep, into this profound sleep actually, and I thought oh that's terrific, I mean that means that he really feels comfortable here. So instead of being shocked I was kind of reassured in this odd way.

Briggflatts is the great love poem of the twentieth century. This is not the most obvious thing in the world because of its big structure. It has a musical element and a certain timing that is associated with modern poetry. I think it's also a great modern poem in that it takes geography and personal history and an incredible specificity of place. But in the end it's about love. Love poetry hasn't been significant in this century, which also makes this a very unique poem in that it uses the modern structure and range of effect, which the academy and the academic mind feel uncomfortable with. This has been Pound's problem, this has been Olson's problem, this has been any poet's problem who wants to incorporate more and more narrative and cast the net wider and wider. And Basil succeeded in doing this in *Briggflatts* in a very peculiar way.

From the Modern Language Association panel
on the Poetries of California

December 28, 1994, at the University
of California at San Diego

In 1946 when I first went to California during high school vacation I was a kind of proto-Mexican—a random member in the seasonal migration to California over Route 66 from the downstate Illinois Colonia of the French intrusion from Quebec into the Mississippi waterland of North America. My grandfather was French-Indian. The high school French teacher came over once a week to speak French with him. He was the master pipe-fitter on the Chicago and Eastern Illinois Railroad.

In those years, all I knew about California was that it was the destination of people who didn't go to Florida or Arizona—they were all from farther north, from Michigan, Wisconsin, or Minnesota. There was a summertime traffic streaming out to Colorado, and no doubt some ski-trains from Chicago in the winter. I never considered, even for an instant, going anywhere but California, and California meant the whole expanse of Los Angeles—San Francisco never entered my consciousness until the brief season I spent there in the late fifties and then not again until the late, now much abused, decade of the seventies.

But my California was before bowling-pin-setting machines, when everybody in Long Beach was from Iowa, when great poets like Chet Baker and the Hefti brothers were reading their charts in the beach towns on long, intense Sunday afternoons, when skill flew like sparks from the fingertips and everything seemed preordained and imbued with a deific verity. The atmosphere, even then in the late postwar forties, had already begun to take on that filtered, cinematic, David Hockney, gotta-get-off-this-L.A.-freeway pallor—but California is first and foremost and perhaps increasingly only atmosphere, so no matter how bad it gets, what's the difference? Oecology has always seemed rather disingenuous in a nation-state so bent on its own satisfactions and rapacities and subsequent distribution to the rest of us, that great, dumb, appendage called the United States.

But that was electric train California—now sunk into the layered mental archaeology of L.A. smog.

Charles Olson's California was a projectivist, geopolitical, expansionist, Bear State "submodel" of continental America destiny. It was the end of the road solely because that's where the road ended. Olson had said Melville's solution to that interstate quandary was to ship out to where the real fruit-eaters marked the way across the whale grounds of the universal ocean. To what next? Well nobody has discovered that yet, and that's probably the point. But both of those authors would have heard the term *Pacific Rim* as some kind of real estate agent's smutty joke.

When I returned to Black Mountain College in the autumn of 1953 following an interlude of drive-away tours of the transmontane west, I began to see California as a final subject and a setting of vast consequences—something way beyond simply an exotic place where my uncle lived in a garage underneath some trashy palm trees. Suddenly it was the poetry of a human stream with branching fork to black-dirt, river valley Oregon and the more dangerous and alluring gold-lust beyond the great, forbidding alkali deserts of the interior basin. Over which, we all know, the Californians dragged their chests full of mementos along with their dreadful Ohio Valley disposition to cannibalism, laboring past an aboriginal people who got by on roots and tubers but would welcome a strayed horse—not for the ride (Ride where? would be the first question), but for the lucky encounter with big time protein.

Sutter's gold, caught in the sand bars above a central valley which ran for a hundred leagues to the south, and from which would spring riches to rival then surpass the land of Egypt. Out of the Westward Movement were born the phenomenologies of our perilous unrest, which change only in their growing intensity. California was simply the terminal posting on that chart. This reality constituted a kind of "contra Naturum" for Olson, but of course, unlike Pound's, it was shifting and complex, not a fixed indictment of what looks more and more like a natural propensity for unmitigated gain.

Gold Lust, Expansion as a form of dementia, Real Estate as a form of terrestrial Skin Cancer, Massacres and Last Stands as the precursors of Monday Night Football. This was a collection of metaphors it would have been difficult to produce unassisted in the late forties merely from traversing the old Lincoln Highway, now Interstate 80, which to the untrained eye just looked like the longest, trashiest strip town in the world, and still does. To see it as poetry takes education.

After the war, in the second, declining phase of the institutional life of Black Mountain, that would be about from the rectorships of Josef Albers to Charles Olson, most of the students had been educated somehow and went to the college to study with a particular person in a particular field. To be educated at Black Mountain was an altogether different proposition. Olson's essays and correspondence directed to Robert Duncan questioning the applicability of Eastern quietism and resignation to an innately dark and willful Western energy were among the defining exchanges of the time and retain their relevance in the face of the fine-grained, type-free logic and generalized submissiveness of the extremely recent past. That argument and those discourses were part of my curriculum as a volunteer in an experiment which was conducted in the very bosom of the most reactionary decade of the century. California occupied a preoccupational position in speculative discussion—and that's all there was around Olson—from the Donners to Duncan. The running argument regarding the validity of the rival psychological systems of Freud and Jung was immediately understandable to me as the Catholic versus the Neo-protestant, and I was beginning to get the glimmer that my education, because I was educated at Black Mountain, was going to have some powerful holes in it.

Robert Duncan was presented as the Modoc of American poetic perception; i.e., you'll never get to him because the carpet of obsidian surrounding his position will cut your horses' hooves to ribbons. For a long time I believed that Duncan's medium of exchange was woodpecker scalps. By the time I first met him I had been programmed by both his own tractarian poetics, and by the testimony of the almost medieval literary road crowds of the period from 1955 to 1965 (a decade that's almost never mentioned) as to his vast, permutational chain of psychological association and parallelism, and his immediate seizure of the moment to turn anything into anything else. I once heard him claim that he had learned to speak while taking in breath so he could ward off interruption, and of course it was true. Why anyone would have wanted to interrupt him was more difficult to understand—because he had thought incessantly about important things which came from the deep past but applied to the present moment, and therefore suffered no impairment of sobriety—like a note Jennifer Dorn took during one of his seminars in Kent, Ohio, just after the Troubles, speaking of the Bacchic rites—"The rapture of the initiated lies in this: his soul is congregationalized."

His sense of poetry was large scale in its grasp of the immediate. When he came to the Plaza to see me in January 1970 after visiting Olson in the hospital, he spied Dennis O'Brien's new book on Empedocles which I'd brought signed from London and said, "What's that?" in the middle of an endless sentence. I said, "I'm taking it to Olson, it's the new Empedocles." He swept it off the telephone table and said, "I'll have that—he won't be needing it." It was such a triumphant gesture of proprietary succession, it just made me blink with the momentum of it. Yet again, the poet is the slave of truth.

What Duncan and I understood from the first was we were both Protestants in the camp of the Catholics, a fact that Duncan reminded me of every time we met. His presumption that he was the son of Ezra Pound and H.D. was certainly entertainable as a function of the muse, but as a literally physical possibility, which it seemed to be, was just too freaky to dwell on.

Duncan was a California touchstone for me all through the years of religious wars in Southeast Asia and the mindless toleration of the satanic spirit at home. We never corresponded, practically by instinct, and we were carefully never confidantes, but whenever we met we laughed our guts out at something ridiculous like "the resurrection in the flesh," and something like abortion and population control was just up to you.

But for Olson it wasn't. Olson could tolerate the license of D. H. Lawrence because Lawrence was religious, and sufficiently anthropological about it to diffuse the taint of the Reformation and righteousness with which his work is steeped. But he couldn't accept the license of Henry Miller because Miller was an agent of the devil. Olson saw that Miller was the embodiment and advertisement of the putative cultural defects he pretended to address in the banned books—the greatest modern ploy of modern distribution, and the opposite of suppression.

One morning in London, at breakfast, after an all-night session (Olson insisted on staying up all night, because he said he followed the rule of the Mayan astronomer of the Caracol who studied the stars, and stayed out of the way of those who had work to do in the daylight), Barry Hall, the publisher of *West*, with Tom Raworth, advanced the notion, which seemed oddly more current then than it does now, that the problem in India was overpopulation, which leads to hunger and plague and human devastation, would you agree? Olson said, "No, everybody who wants to be born should be born. The numbers don't matter—to die off in great waves through pestilence, epidemic and disaster is natural." It was the consummate statement of the Roman position, and not that divergent from the Earth First! position which so angered the sensitives around the "We are the World" inanities.

The other side of this strict articulation of the way between heaven and earth brings me back to the big holes. It is true that there was an Index in the late phase under Olson at Black Mountain, but a couple of centuries were missing—the seventeenth, containing Milton and the struggle to make English independence stick, and the eighteenth containing a rhetoric of defiance and ridicule and a poetry of derision, which Olson correctly saw as a concerted attack on the centrality of authority.

But what matters out of all that is California's national contribution to a line of bohemian scholars which I think begins with Dryden and runs through all the nonconformities like Samuel Johnson and Melville and Browning and Pound to Olson and ultimately on to Duncan and Rexroth and Jeffers.

All the devotees of the master Olson, who were twisting and moaning over Tom Clark's portrayal of him as blasphemous, just showed their lack of respect for unfettered and wild scholarship—it was because of his habits we loved him. We knew he was going to find a Hittite under every rock, but that wasn't the point—the reason the Hittite was there was invariably interesting, and expanded one's sense of the probability of human travel.

But nature in California might be in for some sociopathology heretofore not guessed at. Dispatches from San José tell of the recent unveiling of a statue of Quetzalcoatl in the downtown plaza. I don't think anybody's ever claimed that the people of San José are all that bright, but the god who created man out of maize was also mistaken for a gringo.

No, I think the deity they meant to erect was the prodigious Huitzilopochtli, who would have eaten gringos like they were Vienna sausages, and when he really went to work, demanded the heaviest tribute in human blood on both the historical and the mythological record.

The cure for the creeping ataxia of American Poetry at the end of the millennium (into which we have had such a hurried, gate-crashing entry) is some measure of hauteur, which the great, suppressed Soviets like Akhmatova and Bulgakov had in great measure. California, in its fawning, bootlicking, all-inclusiveness, and in its nurturing of the chimpanzees of critical theory, doesn't look like it'll be much help with this deficiency. But again, that just points out that multiculturalism sacrifices culture on the altar of conformity. The pertinent Spanish word is *desdén*—that's when you turn your back on the bull.

Waying the West

The Cooperman Interviews

*University of Colorado graduate Matthew Cooperman
interviewed Ed Dorn over the course of the 1990s, first and
formally on August 24, 1993, and continuing in what
would become a decade-long conversation and correspondence.
Subsequent interviews took place on September 13, 1998, with
Jennifer Dorn and myself present and on April 7, 1999, in
an exchange facilitated by Peter Michelson, who acted as
interlocutor during the interview process.*

*In these interviews we hear Dorn the contrarian, a man on
a dialectic mission. We hear his late style in an explication of
"Languedoc Variorum" and other controversial statements on
contemporary American poetry and its intellectual fads and
fetishes.*

*In one of his last recorded interviews, as if a final act of
defiance to Roman Catholicism—as if he could go back and
do the last thousand years over again—Dorn expresses a desire
to convert to the Eastern Orthodox Church.*

Matthew Cooperman: You've commented about the American
penchant for periodicity, for calling a decade simply something
that exists between two zeroes. But it would seem the 1950s
stretched to at least 1965, if that's not too arbitrary.

Edward Dorn: That's true. And in many ways, through 1953 was
still postwar. None of the decades line up. It's just a convention.
Sociopolitically they don't play that way.

Cooperman: It's depressing to see where we've come. Our age
of specializations and "isms" seems to invent limits of time and
space at the drop of a hat. Do you think that this compartmen-
talization reflects a personalized perception of history, a type of

reduction in scope that tries to make history simply an index of identity?

Dorn: There is a revenge on the past, which every generation seeks to take. There's nothing new in that. Pretentious terms like *political culture* and stuff are just so banal. I mean there's no culture in politics. It has no meaning. It's the pretense of what's called the continuous present, and to use one of their idiotic statements, denial. The whole thing is ridiculous. Multiculturalism's denial is so monumental, and their refusal to look at the past's complexities so complete, that history has just dropped out of consideration. It has no meaning, and is part and parcel with an intense anti-intellectualism that now rules. So you can't follow history, you can't get a sense of history, you can't seek to understand the whole transmission of human life without an intellectual distinction. And that, of course, is totally forbidden.

Cooperman: Do you think that's just cultural relativism?

Dorn: No, I think it's programmed ignorance. And like religion of any kind, and like the intention of the state, all states, its function is to enslave, capture and enslave. Once that's even partially successful economically, it's easier to run a kind of blind consumerism which is the engine then of a further economic reality that seeks to manipulate on a global level. This, of course, is the meaning of the new "corporate world, corporate globe." And its aim is total control and its outward manifestation is consumerism and its mechanism is ignorance.

Cooperman: Let's talk about *Abhorrences*. While a certain iconoclasm and moral excoriation runs through a lot of your work, it seems very explicit there. Was that an attempt to explode the decade as something we could take seriously?

Dorn: *Abhorrences* was an act of love actually. I mean it took America that seriously. I never had done that before. I must say I never shall again. But I felt that was the corrective for the abysm of greed. I mean, the eighties, there's no question about it, were the moral nadir. The unrelenting dryness and stiffness of the moral rigidity of *Abhorrences* was meant to counteract the abandonment to banality that the decade, actually twelve years, represents.

Cooperman: Are we in any better place at this point?

Dorn: Just the test of the few years we've passed has made a big difference. I mean the human condition hasn't improved much. At least that Genghis Khan is gone. You know we settle for smaller and smaller improvements.

Cooperman: How then has your work attempted to engage history in a constructive and resistant way? Broadly stated, history seems the very engine of your work.

Dorn: I spew scorn everywhere I can. I mean why not? For one thing it makes for an interesting life and that would be excuse enough.

Cooperman: That seems reductive. There's a particular moral sobriety in your work from very early on. I'm thinking of the first three books. There's very real longing and caring and resisting going on. And then, at a certain point, perhaps *Gunslinger* being the pivot, this incredible humor emerges and the satirist really begins to flower. How did that happen?

Dorn: Humor is aggressive and humor is an attack, of course. You can't attack anything with sadness. And increasingly you can't attack anything with seriousness. Humor is a kind of mechanism and it already had, even say back in the days of, to speak of the archaic, back in the days of Ransom. Now I think humor is fit to be pretty serious really. I mean if anything now seems even vaguely emotional, it's gone. It's dead in the water. It's not happening. Not that there isn't a lot of good copy that seeks to do this, but I mean we can dismiss it, we don't even pay any attention to it.

Cooperman: You've pointed out that *Gunslinger* was decidedly different than, say *Maximus, The Cantos,* or *Paterson,* in that those places had locality. *Gunslinger* is an epic about travel, and movement away from the center. It seems to set up an alternately sympathetic and antagonistic paradigm for the epic, of an extension of the idea of the local and of movement out of any central location, which is obviously connected to the whole western motive of travel, conquest, and migration. And yet *Gunslinger* seems to engender some "cutting the epic off at the knees."

Do you think that, while not a conscious decision, *Gunslinger* did have that leveling effect?

Dorn: The whole question of whether it is an epic or a mock epic or a pseudo-epic strikes me as increasingly beside the point. Adjectivally I think it's an epic. It's got epic pretensions. Anybody that does something that might prove to be an epic has to have pretensions.

I think it's secondary and late, and therefore relative to Virgil more than Homer. But all that seems quite obvious. For one thing Virgil is the "out western" way of the thing. You know if you take a regional, located American long poem like *Paterson*, or *Maximus* or one of my favorites, much smaller, and without pretensions at all, Haniel Long's *Pittsburgh Memoranda* to look at it from Olson's point of view, true polis. I don't know how that stuff got translated into regionalism in America. I think it's just a lazy way to look at it and I think it's partly one of the dangers of academic characterizations. This academic regionalism tries to make an honorable recapitulation of life in a place and bring it into the language of poetry. And really the devices between *Paterson* and *Maximus* aren't that different because they focus their material, and their documentation comes from the witness of the past. And obviously *Gunslinger* doesn't do that.

Cooperman: Exactly. *Gunslinger's* conception of polis is movement, is the "constantly sliding away" on the eventuality of "maybe" getting to Las Vegas, and that being a Shangri-La, and a mirage in the desert anyway.

Dorn: Well once you cross the fortieth parallel, or the ninety-eighth meridian, or wherever you want to take the West from, it doesn't matter that much as long as there aren't too many trees around. Again, it's drift. And there's locus, but the locus is where you're at and when you move, the locus moves.

Cooperman: That's always struck me as one of the distinctions between space and place in the West. That in the West there's always a spatial identity first.

Dorn: Well, it's actually in a strange way the marriage of space and place.

Cooperman: Places within that sliding continuum . . .

Dorn: And you are your space . . .

Cooperman: Don't space your place!

Dorn: Don't space me in!

Cooperman: The line of perception in *Shoshoneans* and *Gran Apachería* is somewhat apparent in the book of essays *Way West*. Can you talk about the connections with that book, I mean, as a collected work over a long period of time that does seem a natural continuum?

Dorn: All through *Way West* there's a return to the human landscape. This has something to do with Ed Abbey. I don't really have a male muse, but Ed Abbey functioned something like that. I don't refer to him directly, but I really respected his staring down the weakness and impertinence of his critics. There's this kind of aesthetic and philosophical base from which he operates that I absolutely respect.

Gran Apachería was in his country and I was very aware of what he thought about all of that. It was a critique of the West using the Apaches as a kind of lens. So, it would have a kind of relationship to the later work.

Cooperman: *The Shoshoneans* has a lot to do with an anthropological curiosity as well, an overarching perception, that, at least for me, comes out of the Carl Sauer quote, "The thing to be known is the landscape itself. It's known through the totality of its forms."

That totality is very much apparent in *Way West* taking on the political, social, and economic realities there as well as the natural landscape. That seems quite different than the various agendas of the New West Literature.

Dorn: The overriding concern on the part of most professional western students is gentrification, either of an environmental or ecological sort, and that interests me very little. That war really is just about real estate when it comes right down to it. And that so denigrates my feeling of the West. I don't even want to talk about it.

The Shoshoneans was rather anthropological, and was ahead of its time, and now it would be immensely incorrect. Charles Olson didn't like that book much. He thought it should reflect more of the kind of spatial jumps and hops that were laid out in his *A Bibliography on America for Ed Dorn*. But whatever skills and facilities *The Shoshoneans* had came out of another person at Black Mountain that I studied anthropology with named Paul Laser, and so that was a problem.

Cooperman: There was a rivalry or tension there?

Dorn: Well, I don't know about rivalry or disloyalty. The fact is, in terms of what could be learned at Black Mountain, I didn't just represent Olson's views. Olson's concern and interest in the West, in the Indians of the West, was very noncultural. It would be like commercial and military distinctions.

Cooperman: Is that distinction, if we go back to his bibliography on America, readily apparent?

Dorn: Well that would be different. There you're talking about Sutter's gold.

Cooperman: What were your reasons behind collecting all the western stuff into *Way West*? The title, the way the book is set up so the essays and the verse progress towards an increasingly western exploration, which I found to be an interesting parallel, both of your career, and your use of language.

Did you see that or plan that?

Dorn: Well, it's all the expansion really. Everything follows from The Expansion, and while there were many expansions, it can actually still be seen as The Expansion. This current fraudulent, inflated, phony real estate as represented by the backlash Californians has really just happened over and over again. The Western Expansion was always followed by an Eastern Expansion. When California gold played out, they all bounced back to Nevada silver, and then on to Colorado gold and silver, and later uranium, and that's why Colorado filled up so quickly, and that's why Colorado stole the stage really. Solidarity is based on status, the change from territory to state was based on population. And that population could only come from a rush, I mean that quick.

Cooperman: Something that has struck me about much of your work from very early on is what I would call a poetics of movement or lateralness, a discursivity that has to do with landscape.

The famous quote by Gertrude Stein, "Conceive of a space filled with moving," seems an accurate description of your work. Within each collection, and from book to book, this poetics of movement restlessly tries to break out of whatever previous formation it has created.

Do you think this has to do with a "western mentality," or living in the West, the conditions of the West? Even in early work like "Ledyard: The Exhaustion of Sheer Distance," or "Idaho Out," discursivity serves to take in both the natural and human landscape, becomes in fact a rhetoric of movement.

Dorn: That might be trying in some really naive way to match the expanse of the horizon or something. It's possible. I don't know what caused all that.

I have a hard time with the so-called "early work" because to me it's so very angry. I suppose what I lacked then was somebody tapping me on the shoulder and saying, "Hey, give it a break." I'm not disowning anything, but looking at it objectively, and I think it's possible to look at things objectively, it sometimes strikes me as being a little overexercised. A certain increase, say in cruelty, would've given it a sharper, more focused, more luminous effect.

And if I were to do it over, that's what would happen. It's not to abandon it at all, but to look at it differently, because I can't much longer, really.

Cooperman: Well, perhaps the writings of a young man.

Dorn: I wasn't that young. That's no excuse. And I was doing other things at that time.

Cooperman: From the early books *Hands Up* and *Geography*, which explore the lateralness of western space, to the recent poem "Tribe," published in the *Chicago Review*, the specter of landscape fills your work.

I'm interested in whether you would consider yourself, among other things, a landscape poet, to the degree that place becomes a character in certain poems like "West of Moab," "Idaho Out," *Gunslinger*.

Dorn: Nobody could be a landscape poet in the same way that painters are landscape painters. So I'm not, and I don't know anybody who is. The fact that you create a setting for the commentary as a poem doesn't make it a landscape poem. You could say, "Out there is an apple tree." Then start talking about the death of Socrates. That doesn't make it a landscape poem.

Joseph Richey: So there are no pastoral poets like there are landscape painters?

Dorn: Landscape is not a poetic device. It is a material thing. You can say, "Over hill and dale . . ." Or, "The rain came down in sheets. Every once in a while it cleared and one could see the black soot of a lonely locomotive traveling toward Aberstwith." That's still not landscape. That's just a bunch of words going on about what's out there. If you are on earth, you are on a landscape, and there's nothing much you can do about that. You can get off of it for a little, like Michael Jordan, but not too long. You are on a landscape. It's dumb to take it as anything other than a total given.

Richey: What would lead one to try to depict you as a "landscape poet?" All the focus on the external? The importance of the landscape as a character? Is that how this reading arises?

Dorn: You're talking more about "haunt" actually. That gets to involve the "human in place." That's what Lawrence was talking about in "Reflections on the Death of a Porcupine." Consequently, that's what Olson was largely talking about. Those things are simple enough. But that's not landscape. People have stopped using terms with any accuracy now.

Peter Michelson: The interest here may be in the local, what one calls the local, its particular activity and complication today.

Dorn: Well, I happen to know for a fact that Olson was probably the greatest actual D. H. Lawrence fan ever. Just a true fan really, and he made everybody around him a Lawrence fan too, because he spoke so eloquently and enthusiastically about him and the whole Lawrence canon. I think he picked up most of his enthusiasm for the significance of the local from D. H. Lawrence, because Lawrence has written essays about it. I don't.

I never saw anything that would constitute an actual definition of a direct relationship between the local effects and what you did with it in writing. And I never felt that I ever knew what the connection was. I think it's important to be interested in the proximity of things, but that's not really what they're talking about. You can pick up the spirit of things that are close by and so forth.

I ended up thinking of the local as just what captured my attention, really, what was close to me, and so that's why my poetry and my system of poetry could be described as a dumping ground for everything that I feel and think at any moment. The local to me is immediate experience, because you're affected by where you are, obviously.

Michelson: Here's an interesting thing that seems to me pertinent, so I'll throw it in and you see what you think. Traditionally the local would be subordinated to the universal, and so what is it about that particular counterpoint that results, in terms of modern poetry, that gives the local a priority over that old favorite, the universal, which is still invoked by a certain segment of the academic community—that is, those people who talk about beauty as a universal, which in a sense flies in the face of what the modernists thought, and presumably Olson thought? What's their prerogative?

Dorn: Olson followed Pound back into it in that sense. Pound was a great reactionary and was actually trying to restore a classical viewpoint. And I think Lawrence, in a sense, was parallel in his own way, in his kind of Nottinghamshire difference from Pound. They weren't characters who would be expected to get along. But they were contemporaries in a very real way. Both Lawrence and Pound took their intellectual cues from Thomas Hardy, who was the literary giant of their youth. If you follow Lawrence, to have a true local, you have to have gods of the local. You can't have monotheism. It does not tolerate the local.

Monotheism is centrality of power and total control. Rome sets up institutions to enforce this. Rome has created the most loathsome of institutions known to mankind, the priesthood to see that the Local didn't gain ascendancy without permission. Conversely, the Greeks were way too local, way too loose for the Romans. They set up little altars wherever they felt the spirit. And they had many gods. Theologically, they were a generous people. That's the diametric opposite of Rome, which is very selfish. You don't get to set up your own little god spot. You don't get to do anything like that.

Michelson: The Hindus still do that.

Dorn: Well, good for them. We're just talking about the disgusting habits of monotheism for lusting after control and dominance and bullying. It's a bullying theology. Definitely. I mean its whole strength is intolerance.

That's why E. M. Cioran has interested me so much in the past few years. He was the last of the true cynics. I mean a real cynic in the philosophical sense, not just in attitude, which is what most people mean by cynics.

And he had the best translator now working from French into English, which is Richard Howard. Those translations of Cioran are absolutely beautiful. It's just great reading. This was pretty lucky for Cioran. I don't know that he would have had a chance if it hadn't been for the fortuitousness of Richard Howard's interest.

My natural affinity with cynicism in the philosophical sense is also with the belief that the only way to deal with an impossible problem is to laugh it away. I mean, only laughter can turn it to rags. I think that's at the heart of the cynic system actually. It's the ultimate desperation.

Michelson: The ultimate weapon of the heretic.

Dorn: That's right. And that's why the heretic gets flayed. The heretic also gets flayed because the heretic believes more than anybody else. You got to believe to suffer that much. In that sense, Jesus Christ was the *numero uno* heretic.

Cooperman: E. M. Cioran is an interesting figure of "the outside." What's your take on the controversy over his work?

Dorn: It's pretty complicated. There are certain loose-cannon, irresponsible academics screaming when they hear his name because he's a fascist, when in fact the academics are usually more fascist on the whole. That makes Cioran real difficult to even discuss because there's so much disingenuousness about him. He didn't get prominent enough to really be attacked because the people who could've attacked him weren't smart enough.

And the others didn't have the energy, so he slipped out unscathed really.

Cooperman: His work does amount to a sort of defense of heresy.

Dorn: He was a heretic. But who is a heretic is a difficult question. As I've explained, it's getting a lot harder to be a heretic because it's getting harder to be a heretic against *what,* or against *whom.* The church is still there in all its power and manipulating everything like it always has, but one day it did wise up and stop burning people at the stake. Miracle of miracles. How it ever got to that point is still one of those great mysteries. I suppose that when the gun became cheap and widely available. I suppose that's what changed all that. So the Praetorian Guard of the church, which has always been the Mafia, just killed people. They assign numbers, that's how it's done. They assign you to kill, and if you don't kill, then you get killed. That's how order is kept. In that sense the heretics have now become people not with ideas, and not with revolutionary intentions, but people who simply get out of order. That's what they've degenerated into.

Michelson: What is your sense of heresy in the context of your own poetic mission? I mean, you do that. You take up the whole notion of the antagonistic, both historically and culturally.

Dorn: Well, in one sense this is not true but in another sense it is quite true. I think that poets who collude with the government should be shot. And I think heretics are the only responsible citizens and heresy is the only responsible position, as well I've said many times. I don't consider myself a heretic in any important sense.

Cooperman: But the charge of being a heretic has been leveled against you.

Dorn: I was never a heretic. For you to be a heretic, or to be politically engaged with poetry, you have to have something in mind. I was maligned because I am a true poet, and I love the literature of the past thirty centuries! That's heresy.

Still, it will remain an eternal mystery as to why such an obscure target as myself should have been attacked by the Buffalo Gau in the first place.

I assumed I was attacked because I presumed the right to dismiss their attention to "language" as a rhetorical vacuity, along with its proponents whose sole aim was simply a job-hunting sycophancy. The obscurantist opportunism these sloths hid behind still leaves an offensive residue on the skin of writing which will take a long time to evaporate. The damage done would be laughable if it didn't convey so much tonnage of ignorance dumped onto the whole lingual edifice. About the only good you could say came out of it was it simply confused and somewhat delayed the formless theorists. It confused their attacks on legit texts, and exposed their confusion about real books. Plus the chatbag proved to be largely unhirable, i.e., to do what? Theorists have always hated poetry from any quarter.

Cooperman: Do you think that controversy worked its way into "Languedoc Variorum," subconsciously or consciously?

Dorn: Not at all. The thing about "Languedoc" is that it's a real job. Somebody has to defend dissent, and somebody has to do it in poetry. It's done in other places in kind of a half-hearted way, but to do it in poetry is serious because nobody expects it in poetry really. And it's a shock to do it in poetry, but that's where it belongs.

These people in general really hate dissent. Their whole pitch about "language" drains the history and the culture and the meaning from the language is to render it inert so that they, in fact, can actually become theorists and join faculties as legitimate, and not have to bear the burden of being poets or being responsible for that art. Not that it ever works, but that's the aim and that's why they're against dissent. It's really just an employment service. That's all it is. They should open up a shop on the street and put the sign up. And as far as their Marxism goes, that's just a public joke. I thought that was a joke to everybody. They don't even read Marx or the great texts. Adorno, Durkheim, Cocteau, they don't have anything to do with that stuff. This is a Marxism that's filtered through other bad readers, namely the French, and they use it as kind of an organizational tool, which means, "stick together." But you could do that by becoming Mormon. You don't need Marx for that.

Cooperman: How do you see your work as affecting a necessary resistance to the current political landscape? To the current poetic landscape? To postmodernism?

Dorn: First off, the modern never ends. Where would it ever end? Dr. Johnson called his poets in *The Lives of the Poets* "modern." It was modern then. They're not modern anymore, but something else is modern. The modern is always replaced.

And again we can thank the French for that. Actually that's part of the French take on things I don't object to. I think it's important to be modern. You get to distinguish yourself from your generation. The modern allows that. Their modern, the late great modern, the modern between the wars, is a different thing. That was an effort to break away from an earlier modern, which was called Victorianism, which was extremely powerful. It took almost the reinstitution of the archaic to fight it off.

That's what Pound's whole thing was. He said, "We have to go back to the beginning and do this over again." So he did, taking it up with the first canto of Homer, and came forward.

He was a fascist, and his great friend Eliot was also a fascist, and their comrade Wyndam Lewis, who Fred Jameson so excoriates, was a fascist. And they were not apologetic about it because they were fascists. They weren't Democrats. They weren't Clintonites. They just weren't. No way. People get embarrassed because they don't realize that fascism is as viable a form of government as any other. It's a human invention, and a human choice. You may not like it. The people who live under it may not like it. But a lot of people living under democratic forms of government don't like it. Bill [Clinton] has already spent millions of dollars trying to get the Serbs to say they're Democrats, and trying to get those Croats to say, "Anybody can move back to your village who was there before a certain date." They say, "Yeah, sure, try it." They're fascists, and they like it because it works for them.

Cooperman: So what's your take on the current wave of nationalism sweeping Europe?

Dorn: One assumption that seems to be getting universal is that nationalism is the big problem here. But nationalism actually does a lot of people a whole lot of good. For instance, nationalism can keep out people that other people don't want to live with. Nationalism can impose tariffs to save a whole class of craftsman on the local scene. Nationalism can construct large public works. Nationalism can raise a small army of ready, disciplined expert people who will get to the border and kick the fuck out of anybody that doesn't agree with them. It has many functions that democracy is no good at.

If you want a faceless, rubbed-out, characterless breed of people who are totally conformist, and do what they're told, and have this sort of boring social construct, sure then democracy can do it for you. It certainly will. And it will do it cruelly, precisely because democracy depends even more on a ruthless elite than fascism does.

With fascism, it's built in. It's not even a question. With democracy, you create the elite contrary to everything you don't like. In other words, it's not natural. With fascism, the elite is natural. It's part of it. It's inherent in it. And not necessarily inherent with nationalism. Remember nationalism was a feature of the Nazis in Germany, who after all called themselves Nationalist Socialists.

Richey: Fascism, and nationalist fascism, may be effective over the short term, and in that way be seen as a viable form of government for quick change that's never easy. But the nature of the institutions that sustain it become the problem. The nature of the institutions that a true democracy will breed is more benign, to say the least.

Dorn: That's just because you think that Dow Chemical is not as bad as the Luftwaffe. And that the history of their genocide is not as bad as the Luftwaffe. That's how you could say that. A lot of people share that view. But it's just an argument. Nobody has any proof on that. If you go into the histories and start studying it, it can look rather different. Nationalism can take many forms. Nationalism can generate terrible things. But terrible things can be generated by democracy too, and are, in fact, right here right now. But we don't talk about those things as terrible things because what we've been programmed to receive democracy as the only legitimacy, and not just democracy, but *our* democracy specifically.

Richey: But there is an idea of democracy that predates all the current argument.

Dorn: Yes, there is the democracy based on slavery. That's the Greek model. That works pretty well too.

Richey: There may be the tyranny of the majority but . . .

Dorn: But it's never been as effective as the tyranny of the minority. The majority doesn't have anything particular in view. The minority does. The minority has got the knife and it knows where your back's at. The majority doesn't know that.

Jennifer Dorn: Surely Ed, you have to admit that the idealism behind democracy is much better than the idealism behind fascism.

Dorn: Well, one of fascism's facilities is that it doesn't have ideals. It has models, like the perfect guy and the perfect woman, and the perfect baby and all that. But hell, any advertising agency buys that package or they wouldn't even be in business. That's the whole machinery with which Proctor and Gamble operates.

Cooperman: So you're saying that by virtue of its being more pragmatic, more up front about its aims and methods, fascism is less problematic?

Dorn: I'm saying that there are a lot of stupid people who automatically think that fascism and nationalism and all these alternative governments are bad.

Jennifer Dorn: And communism?

Dorn: They don't even hear communism as a system. Communism is just a scare word. In the United States that was used to cry wolf for so long that it's not even an effective term anymore.

Jennifer Dorn: Let's make this clear. You aren't advocating fascism.

Dorn: I've never advocated anything. I'm just saying that I wouldn't advocate fascism any more than I would the kind of democracy that most people seem to believe is blameless.

Cooperman: So in defending dissent, one is always an iconoclast trying to preserve the possibility of dissent in all cases, whether it's toward fascism, or democracy, or whatever else?

Dorn: Or communism, sure. A lot of heretics were really communists. They were non-Marxists. They were more collectivists, perhaps. But it was a form that Americans would call communism. Doing anything by cooperation is communism in the United States.

Cooperman: Turning back to "Languedoc Variorum," why did this chapter in the Crusades interest you so much?

Dorn: Because of the sites they left all around there. The physical evidence is everywhere and it's just astonishing. In southern France, they inherited the greatest real estate in the world with the most well-built houses anybody ever erected. You'll see a little red Citroen outside a castle that's been made into apartments. They're still using these things. They're literally made to last forever. So it's a culture and a way of living that's still there in a sense.

Cooperman: But that subject could take all sorts of different historical forms. Why did you choose to focus on this particular group of heretics and this particular chapter in the whole history?

Dorn: I'm concerned with all heretics—John Hus, the Peasants' Revolt, the Czech. It's not just Provence, or Languedoc. Languedoc just happens to be the region I was living in, and that was a preoccupation. One of the main characters, because he's one of the world's worst bad guys, is Simon de Montfort, who made a famous campaign through Languedoc. You can hang a lot on that because he was an absolute instrument of the church to a far greater extent, although less effectively and less involved, than somebody like Charlemagne. He was a killer and he ran a killing machine.

Cooperman: Was he a fascist?

Dorn: His orders came from a fascist source—Rome. It's not Berlin.

One of the things that's awfully difficult to take when people want to discuss these things is that there's a lot they don't have straight, like who the fascists were, and how did fascism grow up, and where did it originate, and what were its functions, and so forth. Very little is known and it won't be talked about. It's not taught and it's not discussed. When you get the forms of government lined up in a civics class, if they still have civics class, fascism is not there to be represented.

Pound's influence is enormous in showing that archaic democracy is a form of fascism. There is that connection and it did come forward from 1910 or so, before the first war. It became really obvious that the ruling elites were going to lead through modern industry. There were big changes in industry in moving from steam to electricity. That was a revolution in and of itself. Already the Industrial Revolution was well established, and fascism could in a strange way hide inside of electricity. These figures like Edison and Ford, who were fascists actually, represented an amazing elite of wealth. That kind of wealth is unimaginable now. Some executive shithead running MGM doesn't even dream of wealth like that. And they had a view of what they wanted to impose on the country, and they largely did. Out of this comes light at night, consumerism and rapidity of travel.

Richey: So this is the time when the power elite and all their machinery were being installed?

Dorn: This is early modern, the time of Pound and Eliot and Lewis and Ortega and Julian Benda. It was a very active period when Benda and Wyndham Lewis, who has a very great book from that time called *The Art of Being Ruled,* were stirring it up. And it was the period of the formation of the media elite. Indeed, the media is the elite. They are the masses in the way that Ortega y Gasset the Spanish philosopher said, "The media are the masses." But a lot of people were confused by that. He meant the masses were the technicians, which made it possible for the elite to exist and exercise itself. That's why he called the masses the technicians. The media that Ortega y Gasset had in mind was the efficiency of the police in tandem with the new electronic communications, which was still primitive voice and all wire. But that's what he meant by the clerkship that ran all that. In fact, Benda's book, *The Revolt of the Clerks,* was a kind of companion piece to Ortega's *The Revolt of the Masses.* Those were the people who scared the shit out of them, because they saw for the first time an elite that had an expert cadre of its own which would do its bidding, and would keep it to themselves.

People really thought about these questions. They talked about them every day, and they published books on them. They were a lot more intelligent, and a lot more human, than Derrida and all that spawn, which is really just dreadful.

This is predictable in some ways because you know France always did use the United States, since 1776, to get at England. They could never get to the island. Napoleon couldn't get the tunnel built. They got to the island one time, in 1066, and then it actually became "the island," and not French after all. But it's their obsession.

It's got to do with the language. It has to do with the fact that English always preempts French because it's an absorbing language. It soaks up vocabulary like water. French doesn't. This is why they have come to America, and introduced these limitations, put rules on things, and get people hating intellection, hating knowledge, hating history, and trying to cut down the mental capacity of the academic apparatchiks because that's about the only way that you can do it. Since you can't stop the language from growing, you have to.

Richey: So we can get French deconstructionists in the United States on espionage charges for being deep plants into our language and culture?

Dorn: Well, that's what they are. It's an invasion of the most parasitic, insidious kind. It's just horrible. It's a lot worse than germ warfare really. Meaning and content in print are like not even allowed.

On the Making of "Languedoc Variorum"

Interview by Peter Michelson,
Denver, Colorado, April 7, 1999

Peter Michelson: Tell us more about the origins of "Languedoc Variorum."

Dorn: "Languedoc Variorum" was once titled "Languedoc Around the Clock" at the suggestion of Jeremy Prynne because that was his sense of it. But I don't think he had much faith in my ability to tackle his domain, so he was trying to relieve the situation in some way.

But anyway I finally did land on this method. I wanted a poem that would be multicultural and multiethnic. I thought the only way to trash these ideas actually, which certainly needed to be done, and which is still, as far as I'm concerned, one of the main reasons for doing the poem, is to actually mimic the serious scholarly procedure of a variorum edition. The heretics deserve a multiple commentary at least. I had been interested in the stock market report at the bottom of Turner, the Nasdaq—everybody would know that, and then, Naz being the Nazarene, the Nazz—that was a kind of a Lord Buckley reference to Nasdaq.

And then the subtext. There's the famous charge of the theorists that everything's got subtext and everybody's lying. So that found its own place floating at the bottom. In a true variorum you've got all the historical commentary of people who have read the text through the ages, from whenever Shakespeare scholarship began in the late seventeenth century and through the eighteenth century and nineteenth century. So I found that part of the form to be a ready dumping ground for any kind of off-the-wall ideas I happened to have about what was also happening in the present, concurrent with the text, which was at the top, and ran across the top like in a variorum. The poems are a fairly serious attack on how people who have questioned authority have been treated throughout the ages. This is an important and legitimate subject for poetry.

What we call poetry now may or may not be metered, and if it falls into meter once in a while it could be by accident, it could be by intention, or it could be by instinct. There's just no way to use poetry unless it's constantly searching within itself for a new way to be read. In fact that's what poetry is to me now. I can't understand how people who write poetry aren't constantly or incessantly searching for new manners of approach to the poem, because that's about all we can do now. I don't know of anything else that can be done with it. Sure, you can rhyme and you can think in rhyme, but rhyme that comes in the middle of the line is more interesting now than a rhyme that comes at the end, and that's a consequence actually of the reader having been worn out by several hundred years of rhyme coming at the end. We have no control over that. That just happened. That happened before we got here. But that doesn't mean that rhyme is not useful. I was trying to explore ways in which you could place rhyme in various positions in a line, as in "The Cycle," which is referred to here. You can call this experimental or not.

Experimental in our time has largely come to mean incomprehensible, and I certainly don't have any truck with that. I'm very suspicious of any language that is not fairly immediately comprehensible. I don't have much patience at all with just sounds. I never have. I don't object to having some people do that, and I can be amused about as long by that as I can by a "poem concrete." But that's not very long. I think the poem should be pitched at as intellectual a level as you're capable of. Because if it's not, then you shouldn't be doing it. That's what exploration and experimentation are to me. That's the only kind that I would have any respect for.

Michelson: This refers back to your earlier comment about what Olson is doing in his essay—that he opened it up in ways that his own intelligence could explore. What occurs to me is how breath, for you, was not a particularly interesting aspect of that essay, but for Olson I suspect breath was imperative because you can hear him taking these breaths, then taking off.

Dorn: Well, he had a lot of trouble breathing. He was an extremely heavy Camel smoker, and he had emphysema. The medical aspects of that essay would be worth exploring by listening to the tapes. It's one of the aspects of that essay that hasn't been touched for obvious reasons, but it should be. And, you know, when we're just about to drain the tobacco companies of capital, it could be an interesting question. There's a Ph.D. subject.

Michelson: Another interesting aspect is that Olson is a lot broader, because any given intelligence brings what it's capable of to the notion of "projective verse," and adapts it and just says, "Look, this is an open field, let's run."

Dorn: I agree with that completely. All I'm saying is that he gave me my license.

Michelson: Right, right. And any license also imposes the notion that you know what the rules are by which that license is functional.

Dorn: You have to qualify for the license.

I really got into "Languedoc Variorum" through my teenage experience with going through the rights of the ritual hero, Jacques de Molay, who was flayed by the church and was set up as a heretic by Innocent III. Innocent, that's very, very funny. At least the Huns had a sense of their own importance. They'd be like so-and-so the Momentous. That's cool, you know. But Innocent?

Anyway, deeming someone a heretic was an excuse for seizing the property of the Knights of the Temple, the Knights Templar, and so Jacques de Molay was singled out. He was tortured hideously and finally flayed, while alive of course. That was the ultimate treatment of the heretic. And he was drawn and quartered and his body was utterly taken care of. Jacques de Molay wasn't the only knight to be tortured. He just suffered the most spectacular and sensational torture, death through very slow torture.

The ultimate goal of the Western church is centrality of power. And that's why, in fact, they couldn't stand the realism of orthodoxy. And that's why they had to stay behind in Rome, to make the biggest empire that ever was, the most successful empire, which is still actually largely intact.

Anyway, what I'm talking about is essentially a high school experience, which didn't come back to me until two or three years ago when I started reliving vividly the experience of when I was sixteen–eighteen years old. I was always rather doubtful about, well, virtually everything, because I grew up in a milieu that encouraged a lot of doubt if you wanted to survive with anything intact at all. But still I could see the point and meaning of the Jacques de Molay story.

I interposed a lifetime of learning and experience when I went to Languedoc in 1992. I used to go out after work, at the University of Montpelier (Paul Valéry's university) when I did my exchange, and just wander around, and the idea just presented itself. I mean these little towns, the people, and the density of the Crusade history. When the Holy Army returned to southern France, these were the most experienced military men in Europe at that time, and there was nothing for them to do. All they knew how to do was fight. They were expert marauders and wasters, and they had their practice against a really tough enemy. I mean Saladin had valiant and experienced soldiers. These were professional armies going against each other. This is not kidding around. This is not death at a distance. This wasn't a cowardly, you know, B-2 bombing. This was looking your man in the eye. This was real.

So when I started the poem, there was a serious collision. I was impelled to do this from extremely early experience and passion. But in the meantime I became extremely loaded with other attitudes, opinions, and information that, of course, you wouldn't have dreamed of in the de Molay Hall. It wasn't part of the ritual. You just learned what that ritual was. You wear robes and you memorize your parts and you reenact. And it prepared you for the bigger and greater ritual of the Masonic.

I never became a Mason. Actually, most of the boys in my de Molay chapter, most of their fathers were Masons. My father might have been a Mason, but I never knew my father. He was a railroader, and a lot of railroaders were Masons, especially conductors and the runners of trains.

The subtext of "Languedoc Variorum" covers a lot of what I'm talking about in its rushy information pattern.

Michelson: So as a kid, for whatever reason, friendships or whatever led you into de Molay, you suddenly are confronted with this paradigm . . .

Dorn: A medieval paradigm, absolutely right. That's what it was. It's a play. You learn your part. You get a part and you do the same thing every time.

Michelson: Fantastic. Back to the masque. And it's still with you, obviously.

Dorn: Oh, yeah. We'd go to other towns and do our variation on it, and they would come and visit the drama, this little passion play.

Michelson: The Passion of de Molay.

Dorn: The Passion of Jacques de Molay. Jacques de Molay was singled out. I don't know exactly why he was singled out to the extent that he was. But it's an interesting story. It was part of the campaign. Somebody pointed out to Innocent III how rich in land and money and commerce these Knights had become. But in order to seize it, he had to fabricate their heresy.

Well, flash forward and it's not a very big jump to see that we are fabricating the heresy of Slobodan at the moment. Not all the world agrees with this Maine poet we have as secretary of defense, Mr. William Cohen. And I'm ashamed to say that I'm a poet because he's a poet. I find that really disgusting. But still that's what poetry has become. It's become a helpless use that anybody wants. Poetry is the biggest whore now living, the biggest most pervasive whore now in practice. No doubt about it. And I mean multiculturalism, the whole bloody works right up to the secretary of defense, dispatching our warships against the new heretic.

This is part of the motivation of the "Languedoc Variorum."

Michelson: But it's quite specific in that de Molay was distinctly Protestant, distinctly anticlerical . . .

Dorn: Well, he became Protestant in the sense that the Masons were Protestant, but there were secret Masonic chapters in Rome at that time. And of course Jacques de Molay was Catholic, like everybody was. This was before Martin Luther.

Michelson: So when you talk about orthodoxy in your subscription to Orthodoxy, you sort of transform the sociology of that into a historical context rather than into a contemporary context. Am I making sense?

Dorn: Yes, you are.

This is out of Gibbon. The schism in the church started with Diocletian and ended with Constantine, which is a period of, I would guess 150–200 years. And the Orthodox kept up its tradition. They had the patriarchy. They got rid of the tiara and all of those effects. But they didn't have a priesthood set up to torture and to mount inquisitions, or to physically and intellectually torture the subject. So comparatively, intolerance was not big in their canon. But any religion is intolerant finally. The Romans were intolerant of monotheism because they thought it was a cheap bloody trick. And that's why they suffered so many Christians to be eaten by lions in those arenas. Because they enjoyed it. Feeding Christians to the lions was the literal joke. This is a reduction in aesthetic interest that produces a major kind of culture. And yet they put up with them for a long time before the persecutions. I mean the Christians went around telling the Greeks they were full of shit for having so many gods, and how they were sinners and were going to be damned. Pretty pushy people. Somebody had to resist.

That's another reason I'm into Cioran. He's not just one of the greatest writers and philosophers of the century, he's a resistance. I mean philosophers don't count for anything now, do they? They're not even consulted on the abortion question, for instance. So Cioran's accomplishment is magnificent. If philosophers *were* the keepers of morality, there's nothing to keep now. It's difficult to understand how they just don't count for anything, really. Even poets are better off than that.

Dorn: People who have been robbed of their history, who have no history, who have no moral base, who are the most programmable people who have ever lived in a single nation in the world, in the history of the world, a people who are interested only in shopping and who are only capable of shopping, and whose only product is shopping, are obviously going to be simple to program.

For instance, just think of the duration required to teach them to hate the Serbs. It must have been a matter of hours. When Americans didn't know who the hell the Serbs were. They didn't know the Serbs were not a member of the Axis; that the Serbs were the only lonely bulwark against the fascists in World War II and after in the Balkans. I mean, that alone tells you the whole story practically. Was there ever a population made of such putty? I can't think of one.

As we read it from the recent NATO acquisitions, right down the map—Poland, Czechoslovakia, and Hungary. You have to know a lot about the Austro-Hungarian Empire to understand this current heresy, and the consequences for the Serb people who are heretics now en masse.

I don't see the difference here between Vietnam and Serbia. Now this time it's the West against the East. We're bombing the Orthodox. Now they're the gooks. The people engineering this are Romans. The very word *orthodox* is like waving a red flag in their eyes. Actually, this started with Diocletian. Constantine broke the church and actually removed it, and it was the Romans who became dissolute by not saying, "Sure. Constantinople is the greatest civilization and that's where the church should be headed." And the Orthodox considers that Islam is apostate. And then Orthodox is orthodox; and anything that's not Orthodox is unorthodox. Frankly myself I'm Orthodox.

Michelson: What do you mean when you say you're Orthodox?

Dorn: I'm saying that I think the church should have gone to Constantinople, as Constantine so directed and wished. And I'm saying that I belong to the Orthodox Church. I've joined. And the reason I joined the church is because I saw that anything the Western world so hates has got to be right.

Michelson: Are you telling me you're giving up your Protestantism?

Dorn: Well, I was raised a Methodist, but I'm going to die Orthodox. I need a faith. I'm a faithful man, myself, and orthodoxy is for me. I can bring a lot to orthodoxy. I am a child of the Enlightenment, which the Orthodox missed. I am, you know, a culturally useful person.

Michelson: So when you're talking orthodoxy here, you're talking like a strict historical orthodoxy, that is, Eastern Orthodox?

Dorn: I'm saying the Greeks, who are suffering a big attack by the West on their church, and on their culture—a continuation of the Roman war against them. NATO is nothing if not Roman.

Michelson: Right, right. Greek Orthodox, which is also Russian Orthodox.

Dorn: Yeah, which is patriarchal. You know, there's a saying: when a Russian goes to Greece, he's not going abroad. This is not a cultural war we're having here. This is not about culture. It's about religion. This is a religious war.

Michelson: Oh, for God's sake!

Poetry Is a Difficult Labor

Last Lectures

*These lectures were given during a fragile time in Ed Dorn's life.
Weekly chemotherapy for pancreatic cancer, surgery every three
months for stent replacement, a smorgasbord of pain killers: Oxy-
Contin, codeine, Roxicodone, and other pharmaceuticals, and a
new mix of emotions brought on by his imminent retirement from
the university. Dorn still had a lot to impart. He would exert
himself to the end with no obligation to do so other than his com-
mitment to not go gently and to poetry itself.*

*Original transcriptions of these lectures were edited with Ed
Dorn's oversight. I also conducted an interview on July 11,
1999, to augment areas of interest.*

Ed Dorn: The habit of considering personal expression or
"lyric" as something that strives for compassion with all of the ar-
tifices which make up a poem, is in many ways a loathsome in-
strumentation that leads you into dishonesties and lies and pre-
tenses and so forth that are damaging. It is damaging to the
ability to absorb reality. In order to write a poem of any interest
whatsoever, it should be beyond how one feels, which is largely
a condition that is so freighted with the lack of interest on anybody's part. You really have to educate yourself and the poem at
the same time. That's where it's work. It's labor.

Serious poets are workers. To be a genuine poet you have to
go through the same hoops as you do to be a genuine critic or
scholar. Education is important. Simply to say that you are de-
constructing something aptly means that you're decomposing
it. But if you treat a poem as if it's going to have a life of its own
eventually, then we're talking about material effects derived
from a resilient life. And for it truly to be durable, and to be
truly packed with passion and emotion, the familiarity with the

terrain of the poem and the time and place, has to be much deeper.

These questions are worth thinking about because they allow one to use the word *sensibility*, in terms of poetry. And we can't just do that instantaneously. We don't get to just do that because we want to. We have to earn the right to do that, in my view.

On inspiration, I am heavily influenced by early Black Mountain, where inspiration was a really bad word. Anybody who hung out, around, waited for, expected to be taken, by inspiration was a pariah. That was not how you proceeded. You wrote. Inspiration isn't all that common. The time between inspiration is great. With a poem, you don't get the passion and the emotion without the prerequisite work. It doesn't come separate. It's not isolated. That's one pitfall that poets can fall into: thinking, "I can pen a poem, about any given topic, in a short period of time, and as long as it sounds good and it looks good on a page, it'll wash."

You'll see that the problem with the poem is often a problem reflected in the lives of their creators in general, and in other aspects of their study, and in other fields as well. For instance, one explanation why scientific writing gets so stupid, insensitive and maddeningly irritating is because they refuse to educate themselves in the wider aesthetic senses. Disciplines like physics, mathematics, the traditions of biology always took into account the beauties of scholarship and the sweetness of that labor. What's crept into people's lives now is a kind of vulgar, lazy sense of what you can get by with, to get the most out of, with the least output. Poetry is in trouble, but it's not in as much trouble as a lot of fields are.

Most novels are roman à clef. Take Tom Wolfe, the most popular serious writer in America—he's a terrible writer, but he gets by with it because he's a roman à clef writer. He doesn't say that, but that's the truth. He didn't invent anything. He's the least inventive of writers. Philip Roth, the complement to this from another culture, is a better writer. Mediocrity rises to the top in America like cream on milk, and it always has. If you're a writer who lets those things bother you, you're in the wrong business. If you're going to be a serious writer, you've got to tell it like it is. Yes, it calls for investigation.

Someone like Ed Sanders took a more literal view of investigation. Sanders was very impressed by the Olsonian procedure, and he put it into the investigative mode. That's very useful, and it produces interesting work. Sanders was brought up on the journalistic procedure of the sixties and seventies. He made it available in poetry, and that was very useful. Actually a lot of that got worked out in Boulder itself. That's not what I'm talking about though. I'm talking about another mode that is closely related to it. I'm saying that it's also an emotional obligation to the poem.

You can set out to explicate a type of reality, oh, like say downtown Denver, that you can make a poem out of when it's not obvious that it's very poetic. It doesn't have to be poetic, but you can prepare yourself for this. You don't have to investigate archives necessarily. You're not going down to the county records to see who owns what plot of land at what address. Or you can do that too; that can be investigative poetry. That investigative mode is slightly more limited than what I'm talking about because that can become the investigation of personalities and events and so forth, which are much more specific than what I'm talking about. The general application is to think a lot, a form of self-analysis that one has to do in order to produce a well-wrought poem. It's going to have to be a poem in the end anyway, no matter how much labor it reflects, or how much drudgery it contains. But nobody wants to reads a poem of drudgery. So it needs all the decorative and aesthetic arts that poetry is expected to have—you're not foreclosing any of those things—you're setting up a new base for its legitimacy as a poem. That's the main thing here. And that takes education, and forethought, and afterthought, and research, "logopoeia."

This aspiration or ambition is nothing highfalutin or highbrow. It is common. But it does ask you to think about writing a poem in another way, a way that often finds a certain resistance because the presumption is, "Well if I don't already know everything it takes to do this poem, then why am I doing it? How can it actually be legitimized by my pursuing more material to dump into it?" Those are questions that come to people's minds almost immediately.

I want to underscore the connection with knowledge being the struts and spans of poetry; that is, language intensified so that we're apt to call it poetry—that's all, poetry that is charged when it's akin to excavation and empirical interest in study as much as anthropology is. That's what gives it its power, when it's loaded with knowledge.

I will lay a couple of "documentary" poems on you. I'm not embarrassed to say "documentary" because I do think our lives are documentable. The word *documentary* is something I concocted to try to legitimize a way of writing which frankly and openly and blatantly and unashamedly and unabashedly wants observations and experiences. All writing does anyway, but it doesn't necessarily admit it.

As delivered to Franciscan missionaries known as the Twelve Apostles in 1524.

Nahuatl original in the Secret Archives of the Vatican, edited and translated by W. Lehmann 1949: often referred to by the Spanish title Coloquilos de los Doce Primeros Misioneros de México. This translation is based on Lehmann's German, corrected against binary and other norms of Toltec writing as exemplified in both the Mendoza Codex and the Borgia screenfold. English translation by Gordon Brotherston and Edward and Jennifer Dorn.

Aztec Priests' Speech

What we say here is for its own reason
beyond response and against our future.

Our revered lords, sirs, dear ones,
take rest from the toil of the road,
you are now in your house and in your nature.
Here we are before you, subjected,
in the mirror of yourselves.
Our sovereign here has let you come,
you have come to rule
as you must in your own place.

Where is it you come from,
how is it that your gods have been scattered
from their municipal centres?
Out of the clouds, out of the mist,
out of ocean's midst you have appeared,

The Omneity takes form in you,
in your eye, in your ear, in your lips.
So, as we stand here,
we see, we address,
the one through whom everything lives,
the night, the Wind,
whose representatives you are.

And we have felt the breath, the word
of our lord the Omneity,
which you have brought with you.
The speaker of the world sent you because of us.
Here we are, amazed by this.
You brought his book with you, his script,
heaven's word, the word of god.

And now what?
How is it,
what are we supposed to say,
what shall we present to your ears?

Can it be said we are anything at all?
We are small subjects.

We are just dirt,
no good,
pressed, reduced to want;
furthermore our sovereign here
mistook us consistently
and has cast us into a corner.

But we refute the logo of the Omneity.

We are down to our skulls in this and we fall over
into the river, into the abyss.
Anger and wrath
will be attracted to our behavior.
Maybe this is our moment; perhaps this is ruin.

In any case, we shall be dispirited.
Where do we go from here
in our subjection,
reduced, mortalized?

Cut us loose,
because the gods have died.
But you don't have to feel any of this.

Our dear lords,
we share some of it all.
Now we open a little
the store, the treasure casket,
for our sovereign here.

You say
that we don't know
the Omneity of heaven and earth.
You say that our gods are not original.
That's news to us
and it drives us crazy.
It's a shock and it's a scandal,
for our ancestors came to earth
and they spoke quite differently.

They gave us
their law
and they believed,
they served. and they taught the honour among gods;
they taught the whole service.
That's why we eat earth before them;
that's why we burn copal and kill the living.
They were the Lifelord
and they became our only subject.
When and where?
—In the eldest Darkness.

They gave us
our supper and our breakfast,
all things to drink and eat,
maize and beans,
purslane and sage.
And we beg them
for thunder-Rain and Water
on which the earth thrives.
They are the rich ones

and they have more than simply what it takes;
they are the ones with the stuff,
all ways and all means, forever,
the greenness of growth.
Where and how?—In Tialocan
hunger is not their experience
nor sickness, and not poverty.

They gave also
the Inner manliness, kingly valour
and the acquisitions of the hunt:
the insignia of the lip, the knotting of the mantle,
the loin-cloth, the mantle itself;
Flower and aromatic leaf, jade,
quetzal plumes. and the godshit you call gold.
When and where?—It is a long tradition.
Do you know
when the emplacement of Thia was, of Uapalcalco,
of Xuchatlappan, of Tamoanchan,
of Yoalllichan, of Teotihuacan?
They were the world-makers who founded
the mat of power, the seat of rule.
They gave
authority and entity,
fame and honour.
And should we now destroy the old law,
the Toltec-Chichimec law.
the Colhua law,
the Tepanec law.
on which the heart of being flows,
from which we animate ourselves,
through which we pass to adulthood,
from which flows our cosmology
and the manner of our prayer?

Oooh! Señores Nuestros,
do nothing; don't do anything to your population.
It can only bring more ruin,
it can only bring more ruin to the old ones,
our elders, from whom man and woman have grown.

Let us not
anger the gods:
let us not Invite their hunger.
Do not unsettle this population.
Why should we agitate them
with what we say amongst ourselves?
If you want peace
don't force the people
to see that we are put aside.

Let's think about this.
At heart, there is no satisfaction for us.
We don't believe, nor do we mock.
We may offend you,
for here stand
the citizens,
the officials,
the chiefs,
the trustees and rulers of this entire world.

It is enough that we have done penance,
that we are ruined,
that we are forbidden and stripped of power.
To remain here is to be imprisoned.
Make of us
the thing that most suits you.
This is all we have to reply,
Señores.

It's very strange that the Spanish destroyed so much. The Spanish temperament had a mania for collecting the record and maintaining the record. As far as I'm concerned, aside from their problems with machismo, cruelty, and brutality which are all clear enough, I certainly admire their rectitude with the record. I don't think the Aztecs acted as individuals much either. They were really in lockstep. They were lockstep after blood mainly, not necessarily victory, because they had enslaved everyone around them.

Aptly, this translation was put together by a committee, through the combined forces of Gordon Brotherston, Jennifer Dorn and myself we produced this translation of "The Aztec

Priests' Speech to the 12 Franciscan Apostles." Initially, it was Gordon Brotherson's interest, not mine so much. He learned Nahuatl very well. I didn't. Jenny had learned a certain amount grammar and vocabulary, certainly much more than I, but short of what he knew. I was easily drawn into with just the obvious interest in rendering this kind of content in a language so remote, and the problems that I would be helping to solve as a poet. You don't need any more enticement than that. Having read Prescott and Stephens, this was much more of an anthropological project than anything else.

The larger circumstances from which this text arose grew from an amazing and unique situation at the Department of Literature at the University of Essex created by the rather conservative English poet Donald Davie. Like Charles Tomlinson and other postwar generation English poets, Davie was also a critic and poet, a Pound expert, a very bright guy. Davie created a condition, we'd call it an English department, but he was wise to call it a Department of Literature because it wasn't just English. It was Russian, it was Nahuatl, it was Portuguese, Spanish, and American. So, there were several Americans, like myself, who were invited to the University of Essex as Fulbright lecturers.

The University of Essex is in Colchester, England, an old Roman grain port. It's where the Romans got their grain because the province of Essex is very much like Iowa, or Illinois or southern Wisconsin. It's Dickens country too—Great Yarmouth, David Copperfield, East Anglia from where most of the early settlers of New England came. Charles Olson liked to point out that the great explorer and ship captain, and East Anglian, was a poet. Colchester was a Roman garrison, then a British garrison. It was a grain port. It's still a grain port. In Colchester, I could walk down the street and cross over the Roman wall, still largely intact, and actually know quite a bit about what was going on for the last couple of thousand years. The emotional and the psychological bedding that that gave one to work on was just incalculable. To get connected with something Tacitus was talking about made things a lot more exciting. There was a woman named Boadicea once here who rode into the marketplace and with her sword took off the head of Claudius who had been put up by the Romans as the local deity. So, revolution was in the air.

It was around a very active time, the midsixties. About that time also we were doing something called *Our Word: Guerrilla Poems from Latin America* which were just sent out of the hills to this midwife American poet Margaret Randall who was living in Santa Fe, who I had met years earlier in the late fifties. She supplied the texts and Gordon and I worked one winter on this book, and also began to take up the "Aztec Priests' Speech."

That's what generated a lot of this kind of speech and the interest in it. It was angry, invaded, enraptured in many ways to see an epic fulfillment of a destiny that existed in their folklore. So, it was actually done in a sense.

Gordon Brotherston was making a study of native pre-Colombian languages, including the Nahautl language for work eventually published in *Images of a New World, the American Continent Portrayed in Native Texts*. Right down to the totem poles. The totem pole as text—that's where I got off, but Gordon stuck with it. He liked studying totems, particularly from the Northwest coast, anything from raven culture, the potlatch, the cruelty of the potlatch.

Through my connection with Cambridge, we were able to activate Jeremy Prynne the head librarian, and one of the main poets of Cambridge, England, who provided us with the working instrument for the project, *El Vocabulario of the Aztec Language*. It was photocopied from the Library of Congress and sent to me while I was in Cambridge.

It took the Franciscans five years to get across and take charge and set up the diocese structure and a school to try to transliterate the language, give it an alphabet, on the signs and the sounds, to start producing Fray Alonso de Molina's *Vocabulario of the Aztec Language*. The creation of the dictionary was to educate the children of the higher castes, and to give the language an alphabet and to transliterate the language, so that it could be translated. Once that was done, the main task was to put on record the folk stories and the myths of the Aztecs who, after losing the war, "saw the light," and started to cooperate. Their case was very different from the Mayan across the Gulf where they were punished by having their texts destroyed largely, except a few things. You can't ever really destroy every text I don't think. But you can get big points for trying.

Teotihuacán 1524—that's an amazing moment, when Aztecs finally get to say, "Hold it just a minute. You're saying this is the way it is and you're big and powerful and so forth. But we got an idea about this that's radically different from yours and we can state it." One of the marvelous things about this speech is the unapologetic nature of it. The self-respect of that speech always impressed me as one of the highest instances in this hemisphere of native self-respect.

There were chain reaction amazing moments and this meeting is one of them. What makes it amazing is that it's hidden, and suddenly revealed. The trip to the moon doesn't possess that quality because it's not hidden, and it's not suddenly revealed. Everybody knows where the moon's at, and everybody knows that you can either get there or you can't. But that's a matter of technology. It's not about whether you can find it or not. The discovery of another continent is radically different than everything that had been amazing up to that point. Everything is not amazing the same way after that. I think it's important to understand this breach. This is a matter for poetry. This is not about physics. Only poetry can deal with this. Solid fuel cannot deal with this. This is really about poetry, about the warranty one has as a poet—to recognize what's amazing and what's not, and how it's amazing and how it's not.

The point I want to make is about the call of the creative imagination to do this anyway, and make certain discoveries directly because of its energy, as a result of going out of its energy of the imagination; "to image" a place that you've never seen, or visited in any sense except your mind; also, how the act of researching a poem, and treating it as if it's a trowel into archives so the past sheds a very different kind of light on the text.

I would say that the connection is you. If you're going to be isolated—this isn't an isolating situation. You are the connection and it calls for deep study. Poetry springs from acquired knowledge and the exercise of one's native curiosity. Self-expression as a motive for the production of poetry is almost invariably an interference with the deadening of insight.

And that's one way how to stay sane in America.

There is a temperament that I've recognized in a poet who I feel very close to and who was a student of mine, a Ph.D. candidate at Essex in 1965, who also was a TA in some courses my wife Jennifer took in the Romantics. His name is Tom Clark. Tom Clark functions as a critic and poet through his work. The work produces the cohesion of the two arts. Tom Clark is an example of an artist who has a particular temperament, and he has learned to use that temperament to its optimum.

There are elements of poetry that are so colloquial that you might not even know it. Tom Clark is kind of a paradigm of the readiness to be poetic, and to be able to and to actually activate that mode at any time. But he's also equally heavy on the "anti" side, the antipoetic. In many ways they go together in this world where you create the poem out of fire. Because Tom Clark is a fury of dissatisfaction, he's in a fury. This is not a rage. This is the heart of the Greek cultural weight that unbalances the cheap, spiritual shortcut of monotheism.

Tom Clark is a really restless guy. He's restless but he is a very methodic poet. His book-length poem, *The Empire of Skin*, is the most meticulously verified poem of these times. He can't just exist; he's got to exist in some kind of difficult strained aggressive relationship with his surroundings. He might not like the word "environment," at all, for instance. Why? You wouldn't even ever ask. He's a little bit like J. B. Jackson in that sense. Something that would get under the skin of Tom Clark and crawl around a lot would be Maya Angelou's salary. His eye would go right through that—the injustice of arbitrary worth. One hundred thousand dollars? That's a lot of money for poetry, especially for poetry that abuses the art with "personal expression." But that's perfectly ordinary in this game now.

Student: What's Tom Clark dissatisfied about?

Dorn: Whaddaya got?

Student: Well, it takes a lot of energy to be dissatisfied.

Dorn: It's his energy anyway. Of course, he can do what he wants.

To me it's interesting because it takes away satisfaction, and satisfaction is one of the more obnoxious habits we have to put up with in other human beings.

Student: I think it's dissatisfaction.

Dorn: No, that's a very superficial reading of the public face, the very image of the yellow sticky circle with upturned mouth which is stuck *everywhere* and on *everything*. On the whole it's their satisfaction at their dissatisfaction perhaps. But it's definitely their satisfaction. They are very satisfied. That's difficult to live with because this is what creates a nation of sheep. Baa-aah, baa-aah. "I can't get no . . ."

Student: If you had to pick a time, when do you think we became sheep?

Dorn: I think it was gradual. It's always gradual. It's not one moment when suddenly everyone becomes a sheep, because there are people in what's largely a nation of sheep who aren't sheep who turn out to be the more talented of our criminals I'm afraid. We got a lot of talent and brains locked up just because there are desperate people. There's no question that it's what's happening to the black American male vis-à-vis the prison system. This is a worldwide scandal. We have no explanation for that at all; except fear, fear and ignorance and reaction. Letting everybody play basketball is not the answer.

This has also always been a nation of transportees. Australia got the out-and-out criminals because they were a bit late. We got the yeoman but we were lucky. We had people from the islands who came over and they settled and they knew how to build a fence and they knew how to build stone fences and that's one reason why New England is really there.

Did you know in continental drift, those parts of the country—Nova Scotia and Massachusetts and so forth—fit? If you wind that back, people have found striations that are continuous in Nova Scotia from the Outer Hebrides in Scotland. But the datings are all there in any case. You don't even need the striations really.

Getting back to the point that critical sensibility or temperament is as important as acquiring the background knowledge necessary to have an informed opinion. One problem with untrained critics is they don't know what they're talking about—this is intentional with the evil varieties, and simply weak, half-ass, and lame with the unconscious ones.

People who don't proceed as poets and critics ought to are

demeaning their professions. Doctors, for instance, needn't be as stupid and ignorant and boring as they are. There's no reason for that. There's no excuse for that. They weren't always like that. Think of the great Greeks who were doctors. Think of the great medieval alchemists and whatnot. I mean it's only in our time that these people have become really boring and a burden on society. That's something quite recent. That hasn't been going on for very long. It's because they're not even trying to correct themselves in the way that some poets at least are, whether they're successful or not. Lawyers, for instance, inherit a language of incredible interest. Yet you saw during the O. J. Simpson trial, Marcia Clark and this guy from Boston, and those on Court TV, most were dead boring, yet they were interviewed endlessly. Their vocabularies are truncated and of very limited interest. Their main concern is almost always winning even some part of an argument and they wind up shouting at one another over this. Look at the symptoms of this lack of education and lack of the will to make things as interesting as possible rather than as uninteresting as possible. It's just manifest, it's everywhere. Maybe this is not all their fault. People blame the media for a lot of stuff. I don't know that it's the fault of the media for everything.

Jennifer Dorn: Didn't this happen too with the Sophists? If it was the truth, it was just about argument, and winning the argument.

Dorn: But the Sophists were interesting people. They were the first hired guns of that verbal thing. I cannot believe that there has been anybody among the Cynics or the Sophists who are as low grade as the people you see on Court TV and the people who were interviewed two or three years ago with what went on for eighteen months. Mercifully, their work didn't survive famously among the Greeks. A lot of that was lost. Will any of this current stuff be lost? I don't know. I have this gut-wrenching feeling that none of it's going to be lost.

Where are the Clarence Darrows? Darrow's an example of a lawyer who learned the craft enough to be interesting enough to win big issues. It's just the thing about a poem. You don't get the passion and the emotion without this other work. It doesn't come separate. It's not isolated.

Dover Beach

The sea is calm tonight.
The tide is full, the moon lies fair
Upon the straits; on the French coast the light
Gleams and is gone; the cliffs of England stand,
Glimmering and vast, out in the tranquil bay.
Come to the window, sweet is the night-air!
Only, from the long line of spray
Where the sea meets the moon-blanched land,
Listen! You hear the grating roar
Of pebbles which the waves draw back, and fling.
At their return, up the high strand,
Begin, and cease, and then again begin,
With tremulous cadence slow, and bring
The eternal note of sadness in.

Sophocles long ago
Heard it on the Aegean, and brought
Into his mind the turbid ebb and flow
Of human misery; we
Find also in the sound a thought,
Hearing it by this distant northern sea.

The Sea of Faith
Was once, too, at the full, and round earth's shore
Lay like the folds of a bright girdle furled.
But now I only hear
Its melancholy, long, withdrawing roar,
Retreating, to the breath
Of the night-wind, down the vast edges drear
And naked shingles of the world.

Ah, love, let us be true
To one another! For the world, which seems
To lie before us like a land of dreams,
So various, so beautiful, so new,
Hath really neither joy, nor love, nor light,
Nor certitude, nor peace, nor help for pain;
And we are here as on a darkling plain
Swept with confused alarms of struggle and flight,
Where ignorant armies clash by night.

Dorn: The greatest single poem ever written in the English language . . . by a guy who wrote volume after volume of lousy, awful poetry—except this one poem. This proves that you should never give up.

Student: Who is it?

Dorn: Matthew Arnold, the inspector of English schools, the great critic, now very much out of fashion and out of favor. Yet the schools were well run under him when he was the school inspector then. Under us, the school system passes out Ritalin. Our schools are not well run.

Student: Didn't Yeats write something about him?

Dorn: Well, they were virtual contemporaries.

But perhaps this poem brings up the question of that chink in the wall between the modern and what was beforehand. "Dover Beach" presents that dilemma and enigma for this course. This poem was written in 1867. That's a long time ago, 1867, late Victorian. But it's already projected way past us actually, that's what you can do, the throw of that poem is very great, and it is the greatest poem. The greatest single shot.

I think "Dover Beach" is an amazing document because it shows how a man with a frankly rather pedestrian mind, but a very serious past, could write "Dover Beach." That a Matthew Arnold could write a "Dover Beach" is an extremely hopeful thing in the world. For this to come out of him, that's amazing. It wouldn't be amazing for Shakespeare, because Shakespeare wrote routinely at the level of "Dover Beach." We're not saying anything when we praise Shakespeare. Any praise for Shakespeare is completely gratuitous. For Matthew Arnold it's very different. Matthew Arnold rose above his pedestrian-ness, his commonness, to write this deeply touching statement. You can feel in this poem that it's just written—he's just looking out the window. It's that simple. This immensely great poem comes from merely looking out the window. That is astonishing. And anybody could do it. The potential is there.

How to achieve it? Obviously, you have to have a vocabulary, though it doesn't have to be written with that vocabulary. The vocabulary in "Dover Beach" is beautiful. It's just great in its big-heartedness, from a man who was mangy really. You know, to be a school inspector of the country is anal as anything. That poem is not coming from that place. It is religious; it's a prayer. But you can't write as a Christian any more.

Rudy Mesicek: Why do you, how do you mean when you say that everybody can be a poet? I've heard you say that several times.

Dorn: Well I say that because I think that poetry is inside everybody. But it doesn't behoove everybody to try to move it. I mean, it would be an amazingly alarming world if everybody wrote poetry. How could you live with that? There are still *a lot* of poets. It's a kind of a joke, I mean people make jokes about it. They just do. They can't help it. And that just proves that poetry is a really touchy thing. It touches you, and a lot of people don't like to be touched. And therefore poetry is problematic form. It's bound to be. And that's what keeps it alive, keeps it vibrating, keeps it alive. And in a way, poetry keeps us alive. It's embarrassing, to talk of it in that way, but now that you've brought it up.

Joseph Richey: Do we need a dirty little war in order to write these kinds of poems?

Dorn: Well, it helps. But there is one there anyway. It's always going on. It's just a matter of recognizing it. We are never without war, but people think because they're not personally getting shot or their foot run over by a tank or something that we're not in a war. And that's what constitutes peace for them. But that doesn't mean anything. That just means they're not in a war. Or they didn't notice that the tank was running over their foot. That goes back to what we were saying about satisfaction and complacency.

Rudy Mesicek: You introduced me to a writer that I hold dear, namely Craig Raine, and his *History: A Home Movie.*

Dorn: Because he's outside the culture here, and I think you could probably relate to him, because you're European. I wouldn't get that from an American, who don't in fact know who Craig Raine is, except for the ten, twelve people who were in the poetics course.

History: A Home Movie is a long poem. It's one of the best long poems.

This gets back to the documentary and why sensibility in here means something different than it does if this were a course on Wordsworth. Craig Raine is not a very appreciated writer, but who's an extremely good poet. He's Oxford, and in the American mind, this is a knock against him, as is the fact that his wife is the great-grandniece of Pasternak, and his own family have a Russian background, but not an illustrious one like his wife's. He's just an ordinary. They were immigrants but I think they were prominent Russians, successful Russians. They immigrated because they were chased out or they had to, and I think there's something slightly opportunistic perhaps in their winding up in England. Anyway, from this double relationship with Russia, he writes this fascinating, extremely rigorously executed poem. It's not heavily kneaded or anything like that, but it's rigorously put. And, I mean, it's in tercets, and it's a book of what, 250 pages, all written in tercets. It's a fantastic poem, and a great read, if you've got the taste for it. I can see how it may be annoying to somebody, because of its rigor, not its poetic rigor, but its aesthetic rigor. It's rigorous in its aesthetic.

I'm glad you gave me the opportunity to talk about that poem, because I would like to hope that people here, at the end of this semester keep reading poetry and looking for poetry which is documentary, informed, and passionate.

The Protestant Ethic Revisited

Interview by Dale Smith and Michael Price,
July 19, 1997

Dale Smith and Michael Price were editors of "Mike and Dale's Younger Poets," a small-press literary journal that graced the poetry scene during the 1990s. The zine had the gift of zero pretentiousness, which Dorn appreciated. He was a lifetime editor and aficionado of small independent literary publications, and he generously provided many with his original work.

By suggestion of Tom Clark, Smith led the interview by asking about Protestantism, hoping to gain insight into the spirit of protest that resides in much of Dorn's work, including his work-in-progress at the time, "Languedoc Variorum."

Dale Smith: Would you say that you write from a Protestant disposition?

Edward Dorn: I am a Protestant. I've always been a Protestant and everything I've ever written has been from a Protestant disposition. And it's been against all centralized authority, beginning with Rome.

Smith: Did this lead you to write about heresy in your current project, "Languedoc Variorum"?

Dorn: When Jenny and I went to France in January of 1992, on exchange at the University of Montpellier, I had become interested in the Cathars and Albigensian heretics because she was reading a book on the subject of Montaillou by LeRoy Ladurie. She interviewed him, in fact. I taught two days a week, Tuesday and Wednesday. On the other days we traveled the length and breadth of Languedoc, from Bezier up over past Toulouse. Not a very big area when you're from the United States, but big nonetheless. And France is a big country. There's a lot about Languedoc that looks very much like the American Southwest. You can translate the juniper bushes you see in Utah, Idaho, and Arizona and replace them with rosemary bushes and various kinds of that spicy chaparral. You also can see headlands and mesas, almost thinking you're in New Mexico. It's astonishing. So that motivated me to write about this too.

But the heresy, and the heretics, became a metaphor for the oppression of the state. Because that's really what my interest is about, in the various forms of legerdemain the state can perform to divert the public from the state's only mission: oppressive and corruptive control.

Now, it is very important to understand that the Albigensian inquisition was way before what most people mean by the Inquisition. The latter was contemporary with Columbus. What interested me was beginning around 1209 when Simon de Montfort started marching down the Rhone toward Bezier, where he cooked about twenty thousand people in a cathedral fire at the behest of Innocent III, who made him an offer he couldn't refuse. He was allowed to take everything he could seize as long as he got rid of the heretics. I mean everything: property, people, treasure. No matter what, he could have it. That's a good deal, you know. He could have it all. So he went for it and really slaughtered a lot of people, and many of them were not heretics because he didn't really have the means for that kind of investigation. And so a lot of the people died because they were the friends of the wrong people. A lot of scores were settled in this campaign, obviously.

Smith: What made one a heretic?

Dorn: The Cathars were heretics by definition, mainly because they held that they were perfect. And that's a major heresy right there. And they called themselves the Perfecti. The church can't handle that. They believed in direct transmission between themselves and God, and that's bypassing the priesthood, which is bigger than a sin. They believed in love in that sense. In other words, they didn't need the church, and you could not say that. There were lots of other minor reasons, but when you get right down to it they just saw through the ruse of the mechanisms of the church as a means of control.

Let's face it, every religion, basically, is a control program. That's what religion is. No religion admits that because they say the opposite. This religion is going to give you peace and consolation and it's going to deliver you to wherever it is that you trust religion to deliver you. The West is really into overt authority.

The view of this poem is that the Protestant Reformation was the only revolution that actually counts because the other revolutions devolved from that. 1789 is unthinkable without Luther. The Protestant Reformation made every other revolution possible. It certainly made the American Revolution possible and it made Jefferson's statements possible. All these things are unthinkable without the Ninety-Five Theses nailed to the door. But we live in a time when the Protestant Reformation is not even talked about, or even mentioned, and a lot of people don't know what it is. They know what Protestants are because Protestants are in bad odor now. They seem to get somehow confused with Christian fundamentalists. And of course that's not what the Protestants, who made the revolution, were at all. They were just Catholics who were tired of getting abused by the monks. But I mean, the revolt was no less outrageous because of that.

Smith: What do you think of American poetry today from that Protestant position we spoke of earlier?

Dorn: Well, I think of American poetry today the way I've always thought about it. It's just a gutless wonder and it's totally under the thumb of Rome and always was. Because it admires centralized authority and coercion and nothing else practically, except some cash. It likes the cash flow. And in fact, poetry really is about the cash flow in a sense. And if you look at the people who have made money on poetry they've really managed to say almost nothing. Because the minute you say something, and you can be understood as saying it, and if you design your verse in such a way that there's no doubt about what you're saying, then you've lost the cash. Forget the cash. You're not ever going to be W. S. Merwin. You're not ever going to live in Hawaii. You're not going to be poet laureate. You're not going to get the grants, not the big ones. You're not going to be declared a genius by some board of trustees of a giant insurance company. But if you don't know any of that, you're not a poet anyway.

Smith: What else are you working on now?

Dorn: My other project is a poem called "Westward Haut." I'm pronouncing it "Ho," "Westward Ho." It's a poem of the Great Plains, using I-80 as the kind of spine of the east and west. And then I've invented this other axis which is Lima/Cheyenne. The main character on I-80 is Joe Ochenta, which means I-80.

I-80 was the first transcontinental highway. It was called the Lincoln Highway, and it began in Hoboken. That interstate was planned to go from Hoboken to San Francisco, two very similar towns if you really think of it. But I'm not using the Hoboken part. Just Chicago to San Francisco, because it's the High Plains.

So these dogs, Odin and an Arabian beauty named Saluki, are traveling on this plane and are doing all sorts of deals. And they are meeting Joe Ochenta in Cheyenne. It's like it's the other part of *Gunslinger*, but there's no Gunslinger. I mean, there's no centralizing character in that respect. This is more like a crowd, but it takes care of the other part of the West. It's not the Southwest.

Smith: Is I-80 the focus?

Dorn: I'm just treating it like the longest strip town in the world, which is what it is. There are truck stops. Joe Ochenta is a trucker. There are Little Americas. It's also just saturated with that kind of western symbolism. And it's just like the motorized western expansion, but now it's not covered wagons and horses. It's people burning oil.

Michael Price: How has criticism affected the way you write?

Dorn: I think one of the most felicitous things that happened to my generation was that we had no critics. And in fact, speaking personally, I was able to get on with it and generate systems of poetry that were anathema to criticism. And the motivations of criticism would have been a great waste of time and quite detrimental to me. But for the people writing before me there was a kind of criticism that was formal, and it had an intellectual pursuit that was mostly honorable. After that, of course, it was utter nonsense. Sometimes it's an art.

Shakespeare criticism, for instance in the twenties and thirties, before the war, was sometimes an art. That was about the last time. But that still kept to a tradition Johnson had reintroduced as a skill. He actually invented criticism from his time to the beginning of World War II. And so the last people to practice that were of his school, whether or not they had much respect for him, because after all, he hasn't been fashionable for a long time. But still, that is what was meant by criticism, an analytical look at what had been done with a view of increasing the power of the act of writing. But the war set the big standard for destruction, and therefore a lot of intellection and a lot of criticism became destructive. You can say deconstruction or whatever else you want to put on it. But it's just destruction pure and simple. And it had to do with people's unresolved guilt. This is the condition we're still in of course. And that guilt, I think, is very often derived from intellectual laziness, a lack of fortitude and will, and obviously massive doses of dishonesty. This guilt has been unquestioned and has also been a very convenient cover for lots of cons. And so it obviously infected criticism, as well as motivating it.

Smith: It seems that poets like Gertrude Stein are embraced while others, like Ezra Pound, are found to be inappropriate and offensive for whatever reasons.

Dorn: Gertrude Stein is embraced because she is a big fat nothing. You can embrace this big fat nothing and it costs you nothing. There's no intellectual labor and every inanity you have makes it right and it encourages you to perpetuate all your inanities. She is a slug that should have had salt poured on her.

Smith: Pound takes work.

Dorn: Well you can put in as much work as you want to. The beauties of Pound will come to you without your doing a lot of work. I mean, that's another way that he is tossed off too. But if you want to increase the depth of your perception and so forth, of course you get out the indexes. After all, there's a big body of scholarship. But there's no body of scholarship around Gertrude Stein because there's no reference to anything except to her own fatuous self-narcissism. But that's not a system. It's a self-confirming despotism, actually. It cuts you off. In a strange way, one of the saving graces of this kind of childish petulance, which defines her, was that it never actually made possible imitators.

Because if you were seen to imitate Stein, you would be a laughingstock. So that's good. We don't have all that trash breeding itself. But it does take up a lot of classroom time when people should be learning something, like where Australia is. Anything would be better than spending time with her.

Price: In a way it relates to having a project. Tom Clark has done a lot of research with his recent book on the Northwest fur trade. You've done that with the West. But for me it's hard to focus on a project, or maybe we can't find a project due to laziness.

Dorn: It's not that easy.

Part of the modality is in how you look at your surroundings and how you relate to those things that are part of the political and social environment that you are getting affected by. And if you start to do that, or start to think seriously about that, then you start looking up these other things of the past. It's a good way to get acquainted with the past and it's also a good way to imagine the future.

What is the effect of the present on the future? Which is another way of saying what is the past's influence and effect on us? There's always the future, there's always the past, and there's always the present. That's something that just all rolls along together. And one of the reasons for even writing poetry is to sort all that out. That's the thing that poetry can still do. Not journalism, for instance, because it's a dateline.

I'm a lover of journalism though I don't care for its quality much. But it's something that happens every day, and it really is disposable. That relates to poetry in a sense.

I don't know if I believe that famous statement of Pound's, that "poetry is news that *stays* news." I think that the sentiment is really valuable, but I'm not so sure it's true. A lot of poetry does not stay news, and in fact a lot of poetry is never news, but its potential is.

You have to hunt for a project. It's not just going to throw itself at your feet, exactly. You have to let your curiosity lead you and you have to work at it and you have to read. I don't think this takes scholarship or great huge amounts of reading, but it does take a sort of a nose for it and for following it and staying on it. I think it's a matter more of attention actually than laziness and that people now tend to be extremely divertible.

It's a little hard to excuse poetry this day and age and has been for a while, but the reason I think it gets its legitimacy is for its powers of education. The main thing is that it makes you find out, and almost nothing else in the university is educating anybody in this way. They are teaching how to do certain things, but that's not an education. And in that respect I really think that poetry's the last legitimate thing left.

When people turn against literature and when they turn against their own bodies of information and their own culture; for instance, the hatred of Western culture. Does anybody really believe that everybody doesn't know that Western culture is guilty of a lot of crimes? Give me a break. Of course that's true. And does anybody really believe that by thinking that, you can ignore Asian despotism and its crimes? Well, that's just stupid and that's where people are not educated.

And this is what critical theory is largely up to. Let's say there are 150,000 of these people. As disease spreaders and as infectors of the rest of the culture, they are very powerful because they insist on reading not the text, but the text about the text. And they get by with it and people are scared to death of them and bow down and shut up in their company. And this is a cultural crime.

Price: So you think, instead, that poetry is a way to investigate and learn something?

Dorn: In the end, poetry is a source only for those people who want to know, or to break open their skulls. What's considered your formal education is the preliminary to the long life ahead of you, which you take charge of. Careerists learn well the things that are going to advance their career. For the most part that determines who's more successful than others. Plus connections, of course. Those are quite important. But that's not about curiosity or equating yourself with the world at large in a deeper way. Whether you think of yourself as a poet or not is irrelevant. A lot of people who think they are poets aren't, and a lot of people who don't are. Again it's just this attitude. Because it isn't really a career. I mean, it's only a career if you want to work the other side of the street where the grants are. And that's a great study in itself. It takes a lot of concentration. That's a corporate way of thinking, cultivating those connections. It's not really that

different from being the CEO of your own grant-gathering cor-
poration. You can do that without the slightest bit of curiosity.
These are not necessarily bad poets, some of them are quite
good. But they are not necessarily interesting because of their
success in getting money. In fact, they are very often not very interesting at all, which leaves one to wonder what poetry's got to
do with it.

Through the Rearview Mirror

Interview by Paul Dresman, Denver, Colorado,
August 8, 1998

Interviewer Paul Dresman attended a seminar on the American West that Ed Dorn gave at the University of California at San Diego in 1976. Dorn initiated the semester by unrolling a large map of the railroad lines of the United States, including the alternating sections that were awarded to the railroad builders in the nineteenth-century giveaway of public lands. Works such as "The Book of Daniel Drew," Katharine Coman's "Economic Beginnings of the Far West," and other selections from Charles Olson's "Bibliography on America for Edward Dorn" were assigned. His lectures were so engaging that Dresman became a serious student of Dorn's work and the American West, eventually completing a Ph.D. dissertation in 1980: "Between Here and Formerly: History in the Work of Edward Dorn," a chapter of which was published in "Internal Resistances: The Poetry of Edward Dorn," edited by Donald Wesling, University of California Press, 1985.

With the help of Lucia Berlin, Dresman constructed a chronology of questions in order to create an interview that was biographical in its scope. At the outset, Ed became emotional (a factor of the illness), and the interview had to be suspended a few times while he wept to recall distant prospects of his life.

Paul Dresman: James Laughlin once remarked that as a young man he went to sit at the feet of [Ezra] Pound at Rapallo [Italy] until the Second World War intervened, then he went to sit at the feet of Kenneth Rexroth in San Francisco for the sake of further edification. In Peter Michelson's well-considered essay "Inside the Outskirts," in the special issue on Ed Dorn by *Sagetrieb* magazine, Michelson situates you in a similar way from Charles

Olson's direction at Black Mountain, a fairly direct lineage from Ezra Pound. Michelson says that you then directed yourself towards the opposite coast in Rexroth. For Michelson, this gives you a different orientation and greater potential than if you had only followed the direction from Olson. Would you comment?

Edward Dorn: Okay, well, I didn't sit at the feet of Ezra Pound, of course, or James Laughlin, and I also didn't sit at the feet of Kenneth Rexroth, although I did visit Rexroth. At least in my case, that meant moving a lot of furniture, so it was anything but sitting. But I got a lot from him because he liked to talk and at that point I was there to listen. I found him educated in a way that all my other mentors really hadn't been. Self-educated, but also at the same time more methodically.

Olson was not very methodical. He used the word a lot—that method—but he was scattered all over the place and he was really quite a bebop intellect. That's fun, but not necessarily all that useful.

If there was something worth thinking about, Rexroth could teach you how to organize it in such a way that you could use that fact. And I never found that true of any of my teachers, except him. Also, obviously Rexroth's program, his agenda, was rather broader than Olson's, and his curiosity was much more natural. He was interested in nature and he knew a lot about nature, from the Latin of it to the aesthetics of it.

And Olson tended to have pretty narrowly carved-out channels, like "Look what's left of the Hittites," or to the Vikings or the Oregonians, or wherever. They were pretty specific in that sense. So his method would be you'd get into that rut, and you'd go till you'd had enough, or the rut turned into a sheer cliff.

There was a lot of difference between Olson and Rexroth. I think they actually knew of each other. However, both kept a good distance because they were sort of both intellectual giants in the same way, but also there was this kind of diametrically opposed view of life.

For one thing, Rexroth was an anarchist and Charles Olson was a Catholic. And obviously in America if you're a practicing intellectual, you don't want to say you're a Catholic because it just diminishes your authority tremendously. Catholics have got a lot of nasty stuff in their package and there's no way to get that out of there without its being noticed. There's just no way. So Olson had his reasons for playing that down except in a matter of life and death, like when you call the priest, then that's all there is to it. Except for obvious occasions, he didn't make much of his Catholicism. He didn't hide it, he just didn't bring it up.

Dresman: Why don't you talk about "Languedoc Variorum"? It seems to me an interesting example of what Pound said was most essential for a poet—that is, the trade of having courage. And it is courageous in a sense to address religion in this time.

Dorn: It's really actually a very old preoccupation, simply because the first truly educated person I ever met was a preacher who came to visit my church in what would have been about 1948.

Scottish Reverend Aldridge was the first preacher I had heard talk to the congregation like they were adults. Other Methodist preachers of that day were educated on the whole. But they tended to be pretty syrupy and soupy, and they talked down to the congregation. But this Scots Methodist definitely did not. [Tears welling up.] In fact it was the first time I ever heard somebody actually address a group of people in that straightforward way without trying to make things easy or softening, or "It's going to be okay." None of that. It's not okay, and it's not going to be okay was the message. That was always the premise, but what followed was an interesting sermon about common stuff that you had never thought of that way at all. So, in a sense, the Reverend Aldridge was my intellectual baseline. I also found that this Scottish person had a pretty deep understanding of Midwest American life, and I suppose that he had in his background immigrant relatives.

Dresman: I would like you to discuss "Languedoc Variorum" and that response of jokey but instructive dialogue that appears in "Westward Haut." While I have only seen parts of these long works, it occurs to me that you have taken on religion in one instance as well as another continent's history in the "Variorum." In one instance, in "Westward Haut," you sharply perceive the ethical and moral vacuity of established attitudes in relation to the massacre of the Indians in the embassy in Peru. However, as with *Gunslinger* in the 1960s, your poetry does not react so much as transform the reaction into something artful that is even more instructive than any reaction might be. Would you care to comment?

Dorn: Well, in the first place, I consider that last statement quite a compliment—thank you very much.

The religious aspect of the "Languedoc" poem is partly to work out some personal problems of my own. But the subtext obviously is where I'm having my fun, I suppose, as being a kind of a sociology of post–World War II. This is my way of dealing with the French invasion in a sense, because it is sociology and that's what they are—the sociologists. You see I'm completely baffled as to why Language poets call themselves poets when they don't need that word, which has actually rather become a kind of demeaning and laughable term now, anyway. And why they do this I don't know.

Dresman: I noticed that when Peter Michelson was talking with you, he situated you very well. One of the things that he said is that your concern with the local as well with the contemporary event always connects with history. And that is partly, I suppose, an inheritance through that lineage from Pound, Olson, et cetera. He also said that rather than being an explainer, what you were was a revealer. And I suppose that you would probably think in the same terms about Ezra Pound.

Is that correct?

Dorn: First, one of the most hateful statements that I think Gertrude Stein made, and for which I loathe her, was what she said about Ezra Pound being a village explainer. That is such a cheap shot. I mean it is maybe the cheapest shot of the twentieth century. I don't object to the actual diction so much as the intention of it. The idea that she would presume to put herself in judgment of Ezra Pound is really offensive to me. But a revealer? I don't know if I trust a revealer any more than I trust an explainer.

The fact is, Ezra Pound, through good hard sweat and labor, had learned a lot of things that almost anybody needed to know. And I don't see anything that Gertrude Stein had to offer that anybody needed at all. I never needed one syllable of her total oeuvre, and I still don't.

Dresman: You moved throughout the American West in the 1950s and early 1960s—Sante Fe, Seattle, San Francisco, Pocatello. You held various jobs from logging to firefighting to waiting on tables. You also found time to complete the first books— *Hands Up, Idaho Out,* and *The Shoshoneans.* These must have been intensive, instructive, and often difficult years. Although you spoke bravely in the early interview with David Ossman about not feeling isolated, about having equal access to information, the chance to go to England must have been a huge relief.
   What did England grant you?

Dorn: Well, it made it impossible for me to never appear so brave again. It changed my life, radically, because, when it comes down to it, you can only get so much from books or your own experience. Other people have to guide you, other kinds of people.
   I don't know what this strange relationship we maintain with England is. On the one hand there's this loony Anglophilia that loves the Queen and can't quite realize that Fergie is a total idiot. On the other hand, America hates England, and there's a great deal of Anglophobia. I didn't have any problem with the English at all. I had problems with a kind of political and economic relationship that I saw other people blinded by, and unable to sort out. So you get a certain kind of bitter float, at the same time England was a vast relief, and an incredibly sociable scene.

Dresman: When you speak about the *North Atlantic Turbine* and *Geography* as books, you were talking about larger issues that probably were beyond England, but didn't the fact of being there perhaps give you the opportunity to be cosmopolitan enough to address those things?

Dorn: Well, maybe, although that took a while, and getting out of Idaho after five years would cure you of anything. You don't have to be special or peculiar or odd or anything to not have that as a relief. Idaho is an extremely uncongenial place in a way. If I hadn't left Idaho at that time, with that destination, I can't imagine life.

Dresman: James K. Elmborg's recent book-length study *Gunslinger: A Pageant of Its Time,* a study of *Slinger* in the sixties, has performed several services. For example he discovers the origin point of *Gunslinger* to have been in the mimeographed magazine *Price* that was done by a young Tom Clark, not in *The North Atlantic Turbine,* as was previously assumed. Is that true?

Dorn: That's true.

Well, back again to England, at the University of Essex, Donald Davie was the head of the new Department of Literature, and he brought his brighter students as his battery or brigade of TAs. He brought Tom Clark and others over to be his TAs. Well, then once, twice, thrice, dice, lice, mice, whatever it was, it was an interesting magazine from the Department of Literature on their mimeograph. It was hand-cranked, it was labor-intensive. And there were other things there that were not just Tom Clark's magazine, but people had other projects.

Dresman: Was Raworth there at that time?

Dorn: It was '67? He came then the year after I was there? I thought there were two years. Anyway, be that as it may, Tom Raworth was hatched in Donald Davie's and my brain as the first student in England invited to do an advanced degree without having done a lower degree.

Dresman: Elmborg raises concerns about the possibility that you felt isolated in England in the 1960s and were anxious to get back in order to reconnect yourself to what was going on in the United States. Would you like to respond to that?

Dorn: Well, sure, that was a factor, but it was not a great factor, because actually I did get back several times. And I felt more in touch with U.S. politics.

What most Americans don't realize is that, for instance, the My Lai debacle and scandal was known in Europe eight months before it was in America. And Europeans on the whole were asking, "What's going on? Why aren't they being told? What is this?"

It's a testimony to the efficiency of voluntary censorship. Because there is no censorship—you don't have to have censorship if you're willing to do it yourself. You don't need a censor.

Why pay a censor? No paper would print it until word came down from the State Department, after eight months. But stories like that would get in the *Observer* and the *Times*.

After all, England's a metropolitan country; it has like five or six major newspapers, plus the famous tabloid press, which is a separate entity altogether, or it was until [Rupert] Murdoch bought them all. One of those papers covers the world. If it's happening, they report it.

That is an advantage of no longer being an empire—you can print more. America was still being an empire when My Lai happened, and it couldn't do it. There are certain things empires can't do. It can't tell the truth for one thing, and report it. No way.

So in that respect, I didn't suffer at all being in England. I became much more informed. A lot of my correspondence was like, "Do you realize that all the rest of the world is talking about this fantastic massacre that went on in Vietnam?" "What are you talking about?"

There is this fact that American culture is extremely compartmentalized. The difference between what San Francisco knows, and Salt Lake knows, and what Phoenix and what Kansas City knows, and what Chicago knows, and what Nashville knows, is almost indescribable. This country is more like a galaxy than it is like a country. I mean they can see each other out there, and Nashville knows where New Orleans is, and on any given morning you wake up and you might hear it on the radio, but if you don't, you miss it.

In London you don't miss anything. You can't. On your way to work the front page is there on every block you see, going down to the Tube, people telling you, hoping you buy it. It's everywhere. There's no avoiding it. You can't be unaware. It's not allowed. It's not even not allowed. I mean it's just not even possible.

Dresman: Maybe another point that Elmborg raises is similar. Throughout the book he refers to the Digger papers because he sees a parallel, and there is a parallel obviously between that kind of street theater disruption that the Diggers manifested and the same kind of disruption of normal language and expectations that you're accomplishing in *Slinger*. But you would have had in Europe access to something that was the European equivalent of the Diggers which would have been the Situationists. Wouldn't you have had, and is that an influence upon, or are these just parallel manifestations of the Zeitgeist of the sixties?

Dorn: No. What you're saying is true, with the added proviso that the Situationalistas were aware of that history, but you'd also be living on the ground of the actual first Diggers. The seventeenth-century Diggers.

I first knew about the Diggers from Christopher Hill, an Oxford historian, social historian whose work was on demand and required at Essex. The Diggers were a dissenting group, and they were all over and they were laying claim on wasteland, what was called the wasteland. The wasteland was not what we call waste is like a dump or something, but wasteland was something that nobody's apparently using. Maybe it's owned, or maybe it's not, or the Queen might own it, but maybe that nobody's paying attention to it and letting it go to rack and ruin. So the Diggers' program was essentially to occupy that, grow their own food, become independent as churches. These were all church people. But the church then had a function that was very proactive. They were actually going to dig up the land and plant seeds in it. And they were going to go grow their food. And they called themselves the Diggers.

If you're interested in them you should read Christopher Hill because he's the fastest, most available, most intelligent, best read on the Diggers. They're very important. They're more important than the Quakers, the Shakers, the Methodists, and all those others because the Diggers went after the property. That was one thing that is not allowed.

Dresman: One of Elmborg's arguments concerns Book 3, the *The Winterbook*. He says that it's not merely seasonal but a close representation of the era when the hopeful spirit of the 1960s was fragmented. Everything from the power struggle in Drop City to Nixon, to the inward turning of spiritualism to replace the outward movement of the community is reflected in the language and disruptions of narratives in this book.

Do you agree?

Dorn: I do totally. It's like *The Winter's Tale*—"How like a winter hath my . . ." For its bleakness, it's the time of reflection and the renewal in the sense that what has died is preparing to be re-born. It's the most lyrical book, too. It tries lyric like Melville's chapter [in *Moby-Dick*] "The Try-works." It tries lyric.

Dresman: Do you recall any particularly important and well-received reading of *Gunslinger*?

Dorn: Oh, God, I don't know. I suppose it was a big moment, Book 4, at the museum in downtown San Francisco [1974?].

Dresman: Do you think that sometimes the audience at poetry readings fails the poet or can't catch up with the poet?

Dorn: Well, I think that on the whole poetry audiences have been too tolerant. In the early days, like fifties and sixties, they were so hungry for any human kind of transmission that it didn't always matter.

It seems to me that rap and performance has come a long way. Getting the text out of the way has relieved the audience of that kind of presumed burden that they took on by seeing the text, even manifested by the back of it. Of course there are good readers and bad readers, and in a certain way Americans, as rude as we are, we seek to make a reputation of being on the whole rather polite. We're getting less so.

Whereas Europeans are quite impatient and participate with their own kind of cynicisms and so forth. If you don't get the crowd with you pretty quick, you're going to get a response from them that is going to be disruptive and it's going to make a resistance, which against you're going to have a problem keeping everything balanced. But now I think poetry readings are pretty much a habit. I think they're still good. I think they're still necessary. People still, on the whole, want them. I think rap is very over-rated, but some of it is pretty good. Snoop Doggy Dogg really amuses me a lot. I haven't heard any recently, but I don't know how great it is. It's not that I'm against violence or even against misogyny in music or anything, actually. I'm not against anything. In fact, I'm against being against anything, if I'm against anything. So that's not my problem with it, but it can be pretty stupid and it's easy advocacy of really boring shit. I don't think, generally speaking, that anybody in America, anybody, is owed anything. And when you get forms based on an implied debt, I think that's whistling up a stump as far as I'm concerned. We're all sinners and we've all done wrong and we all came from somewhere else, including everybody.

Did you follow that Kennewick Man story off the banks of the Columbia River?

Dresman: Yes.

Dorn: You would have. Well, think about it. Kennewick Man was heavy duty. He walked across the North Atlantic. This is confirmation of *North Atlantic Turbine* if I ever had it.

The Last Interviews

Interviews by Iain Sinclair, December 22,
1998, and August 2–3, 1999

Ed Dorn's time in England from 1965 to 1970 was formative,
and he became one of the few American poets with a transat-
lantic following. The literary circle that took shape in those years
included some of Dorn's closest friends: Donald Davie, who in-
vited Dorn initially as a Fulbright lecturer, Jeremy Prynne, critic
and scholar who accompanied him to England, Gordon Brother-
ston, a Latin Americanist with whom he collaborated on trans-
lations for thirty years, Tom Clark, an American and the closest
to a literary cohort that Dorn ever had, and Tom Raworth, with
whom he had corresponded since 1960. While teaching at Essex
he met his wife of thirty years, Jennifer Dunbar Dorn.

His English audience was dear to him, as reflected in the
emotional presentations he gave at the Diorama in London and
later in Bristol during his last public readings and interviews.

Iain Sinclair: In your poem "The Impeachment on Decadron"
amid Clinton and Iraq and the economy, your appearing there
was like the persona of the poet. I thought it was strange. It was
happening in this little black box and not in St. Paul's Cathedral
or something.

Ed Dorn: Well, I never had a venue of that kind of scale ever in
my life, but, I mean, I've always been a little black box in a way.
I think the fact that we couldn't find it was interesting.

Sinclair: You said sometime back that the business of the poet
was to keep clear of government and all its sort of pertinences
and privileges and be something else.

Dorn: Oh, I believe that. I believe that the NEA has done irreparable damage to whatever American poetry was. And it was even in my time it's been undergoing a process of definition, and I think that you have to be defined.

But on the other hand the responsibility of the poet is to always make it known that there are policy expressions possible outside the state. And that it's sometimes more accurate.

I find that the ignorance of the State Department, for instance, and the moving of the whole national security apparatus into the basement of the White House are extremely provocative. That started before Kissinger, but I think it became final under Reagan. So by now Madeleine Albright is an obvious figurehead. Anybody who doesn't understand that is misreading American history.

Sinclair: It's quite a strange construct.

Dorn: These people constantly refuse to face the fact that a relationship with Islam is by definition religious. It can't be anything else because they don't recognize anything else. And there's nothing anybody can do about that, except know it. It's important to know it. But I don't see any indication that the State Department knows it. Their ignorance is comparable to the ignorance of the Indian Bureau, the U.S. Army and Interior in their war on the Apache. So *Recollections of Gran Apachería* is still an appropriate piece to read in that respect.

Sinclair: Very much so. The point you make about the only chance to save Slick Willie [Clinton] would have been if he'd been brought up by Apaches.

What were the two conditions of desert life: abstinence and endurance?

Dorn: Yes. Abstinence and endurance.

If Bill [Clinton] were to survive, which he is not meant to, survive that is, he won't survive. But if he could survive, it would be because of those two words. Abstinence and endurance.

Had he been educated not at Oxford, but say by the Apaches. If his mother had given him away to the Apaches when he was an infant, he'd survive. And we would now be a proud people.

Sinclair: Do you think he's kind of the end of the line? Is this the sort of ultimate track?

Dorn: Well, I will certainly hope and pray that he's the end of the line. The end of that line. He has an interesting line. Arkansas was provocatively placed on the trail from Texas to Kansas City. That's the early traffic in cattle and all its various parts, tripe and sowbelly. So all that kind of heavy protein chain traffic from Texas and then Kansas City and then Chicago all went through Arkansas. Arkansas was known to be an extremely dangerous place, full of cannibals, and extremely questionable people.

Sinclair: We went to a place called Bastrop, Texas, to visit an English writer called Mike Moorcock who, for some mad reason, has transplanted himself to this town just outside Austin. He's written about a whole change of consciousness going from a Californian consciousness to a kind of Texas state of mind.

What about Texas?

Dorn: It's a powerful power point in American life. The whole of Texas Territory, if you look at the old maps, its reach was wide. In fact, there was a corridor which looks like what we call a panhandle, which led all the way to Montana. Colorado was once part of Texas. And that's where the last cattle drives were after the rail had reached Dodge City. Larry McMurtry covers a lot of that in his big plains novels he writes. His maps of it are quite good.

Texas and California share this status of having been republics—California very, very briefly, and Texas for nine years or so. When you go to California you really become aware of certain Texans and a very strong relationship between Texas and California. And I think it's because of their size and their sense of subnationhood. They have the economies of nations and California has the personality of a nation in a way. And Texas definitely feels that it's an entity unto itself. Texas definitely rules itself. It is jealous of its power and status, and it keeps a very cautious eye out for any threat to that, for sure.

Sinclair: West of Texas is New Mexico. The most particular quality of your *Recollections of Gran Apachería* is the desert itself and the high desert of New Mexico.

Dorn: Well, the desert is a testing place. People have revelations and visions in the desert, because it's a place of extremes. Dehydration is always a threat.

Sinclair: You've located yourself north of all that in Denver.

Dorn: Well, Colorado is the northernmost part of American Southwest. Denver is a thousand miles from everywhere. I've located myself there partly by design and partly by fortuitous circumstance. It was a High Plains railroad center. Economically, it's kind of an extension of Chicago. The brick warehouse architecture now being converted to lofts is the kind of thing that happens to towns that boom, then their pasts become appreciated again in another sense. They have fine buildings in Denver. They're out of Louis Sullivan, Frank Lloyd Wright, Elijah Root school of architecture. There is something a bit Roman about them. The brick is not Roman brick, but they use brick in that structural sense. It's an interesting town.

Sinclair: Why did you feel the need to go to Rome?

Dorn: I wanted to see the Pantheon, because I felt I needed to do that, and also because having carried on this campaign to re-instill a respect for the Reformation, since everybody feeds off of it, and everybody owes it. Whatever we owe, we owe to the Reformation in my view, yet it gets really short shrift.

Sinclair: How fiercely did you want to chase after that Cathar-heretic strain, because it seems to have been there even in Pound and Eliot.

Dorn: Well, I think it's kind of the underlay for the modern idea, and the attempt, and Pound's blatant attempt, to return things to the classical mode and to instill those motives for writing. I think of *Recollections of Gran Apachería* as being definitely a Doric poem and energized by that sense of the legitimacy of warfare. I find that gone from the postmodern sense entirely, and the denial of those legitimate motives of the past.

Before Languedoc, I always had a thing about the Apaches, because their rejection of European values and European existence actually was total. Total. And their hostility was total. A lot of Indians got called hostiles, but no Indians were more hostile than the Apaches. And the Apaches were absolutely unapologetic about their primitiveness and their ruthless measures to survive and to exist alongside the juggernaut of what they could see. They were smart, they are . . . well, no, were . . . they don't exist anymore in the sense in which I'm speaking of them. That they saw this juggernaut as un-irresistable. They saw that. They probably didn't see the use of the telephone. But, a lot of people didn't.

American Indians are not ordinarily thought of as intellectual entities. But I believe their great skills and intuition about the military arts was, in fact, intellectual. And their culture was devoted to survival. So the paideuma of their children . . . their educations were in the military arts.

Recollections of Gran Apachería was a book done for my own relief. The Indian population, the native, the North American Native Indian population doesn't have any bigger clue to what's going on than anybody else quite frankly, and their behavior over Kennewick Man is certainly proof of that. *Recollections of Gran Apachería* is addressed to white people, not to Indians. I mean, I don't need to, or care to, or don't intend to address Indians. I mean, they're not my business. But attitudes exhibited and displayed from my own race are my business, and that's the business of any poet. So I have a right to that title and it's a serious title. *Recollections of Gran Apachería* are intellectual recollections based on a certain amount of travel through that domain, but also just paying attention to the literature, which is the record.

Anyway I thought, and I do think, that it was important for me to go and see Rome. It's much more plotted and conglomerated than I had dreamed. The obvious superiority of the pagan over the Christian emptiness was simply verified.

Sinclair: It seems the antithesis to Victorio and Apache in a kind of absolute pagan opposition to civilization in all its forms. People don't talk about this opposition to all that was supposedly civilized, and which Rome, in a way, represents in the ultimate form.

Dorn: And still does as far as I can tell. It's still the ruler of the world.

Sinclair: The papacy?

Dorn: I think so. Look at the way the church gets by with palming itself off as an abused minority. It's just remarkable, actually. And the way it escapes all the censure that's directed at the northwestern European corner, which has to take all the blame for everything. And then how it still manages to set itself up as the judge of these things. I mean, if anybody needed any further proof.

Actually, Bill Clinton again is a good example and an interesting case of psychotic confusion. The mode he most admires, and the sense of church he has, he says all the time is Jesuit. He may be Southern Baptist by birth and bloodline and reality, but by inclination and what he most admires is the most diabolical of all those forms, being the Jesuit.

Sinclair: So this becomes then a Crusade again, in an insane way.

Dorn: Well, he is a volunteer agent for that kind of duplicity and so forth. How could someone openly believe that the cowardliness lodged in a policy that would take up President Bush's actions in Iraq which were really only to protect his private family's interest in offshore oil leases, which I take it as known by everyone; that Neal Bush and Jeb Bush and all the Bush boys hold the majority of the offshore oil leases of Kuwait. In other words, that was a personal war.

Sinclair: No, I didn't realize that.

Dorn: Oh, yeah. He got to use the machinery of a great power to protect a private interest. I mean it's quite amazing, actually.

Sinclair: Frontier consciousness again.

Dorn: Absolutely.

Sinclair: It's like Allen Dulles as well. All the research from Switzerland with his money, and its ties to German conglomerates. They were financing Nazi Germany from 1933 onwards, and his brother was sitting on the board of I. G. Farbens until 1941.

Dorn: Yes, what you're saying are the actual details that people often refer to as though they don't know what they're talking about. Every once in a while, I don't know if it's the Jews who bring it up themselves, or somebody on their behalf, but what you're talking about is mentioned once in a while but always as just some anonymous kind of cast of characters who actually did these things. But that's about as far as it gets.

Sinclair: Yeah, as long as you keep it anonymous, it's *X-Files* and you can watch it as a TV show. And the names and the dates and the places start to come up. I was amazed to discover that all through the war the head of the Bank of England was still having meetings with people in Germany and Switzerland, and they were giving money to the Germans. It's quite unbelievable. Banking is above everything.

Dorn: That puts a new twist on war profiteering. One usually thinks of the scrap dealers and things, but the bankers . . . that's another form of scrap altogether.

Speaking of which, in terms of petty details in that respect, the operation of money in Rome with the lire being something like 1,700 to the dollar, and quite a bit more to the pound, coming on not quite twice as much, the speed at which they expect you to make these negotiations is just totally impossible for people who are used to bigger units of money. And they stand about hurrying this process up, virtually reaching into your billfold to extract the money while they have this fantastically powerful eye thing going on. It's not just into your eye, but it's into your things, too, into your billfold, into your pocket, into your shirt, into your whatever. It's just astonishing.

When you think of the British Empire, which was a formidable thing indeed, and, of course, on a scale much grander than the Roman, but time-wise, just like a spot compared to the Roman.

Sinclair: The American empire even less, I think.

Dorn: We never quite had an empire. We always sort of rented one. The Philippines were really never our colony.

Sinclair: What about the whole of South America and Central America?

Dorn: Well, that's a linguistic and economic subjugation that is widely resented in those places. Their resentment is a little hard to stomach too when you think of the nature of those states as being simply the Catholic Church plus whatever military will cooperate. That's the history of government in Latin America. I mean, there've been gestures: there's been a Bolívar, sure, and a Benito Juárez, that's true; but, on the whole . . .

Sinclair: Anytime anyone tries a substantial gesture against, then, CIA moves into Chile and all that stuff starts going on.

Dorn: So therefore, the native energy of resistance, like the Apaches, and I only find their resistance to be absolute, is the only aesthetically energetic construct in the continent actually. The military arts are "arts" at that level. They really are arts. I mean, when you sacrifice your own children, for instance, to avoid the notice of a passing band of soldiers. In other words, when your concentration is that gross.

Sinclair: It's an absolute condition.

Dorn: Absolute.

Sinclair: It is also linked to place.

Dorn: That's right.

Sinclair: And it's interesting what you say in Victorio's battles were fought over the same territory which is now that kind of *X-File* alien landing secret state stuff that goes on in America. It's the same piece of land.

Dorn: This is true.

A couple of weeks before I left to come here, I got a letter from Karl W. Laumbach, an archaeologist who works for Human Systems Research in Las Cruces, New Mexico. He's picking up the shell casings from the Hembrillo battlefield on a site in the White Sands Missile Testing Range. Through a musician named Garland from New Mexico, who now abides more or less all the time in Mexico, who wrote a couple of little suites—one called "Victorio," after those portraits in *Recollections of Gran Apachería*. Lombach is saying that my statements about Victorio are interesting because they, in the poetic sense and I really don't know exactly what he means by this, but they verify and confirm his own work about the placement of the artifacts and the relics of the battle itself, which he's digging up and scouring the ground for. And I thought this is just amazing. I'm not saying that I'm any closer to the truth, or have any special insight into this at all. I'm just saying that the faith in poetry as an instrument off maintaining the past is legitimate.

Sinclair: What you're talking about with that actually, and when you understand that consciousness, then poetry is a legitimate instrument in terms of song and in terms of ritual, that puts you onto the grand curvature of everything. I mean, you've done it. And when you've done it right, all the results and proofs will prove you to be right. Hawkins's equations preceded the discoveries of the black hole.

Dorn: Yes.

Sinclair: It's like a high form of composition that the illuminati have always been able to do, and I think you have been elected to that body.

Dorn: Whether I am or not, I'm very happy that you're a witness to how I feel about it.

August 3, 1999

Dorn: Once, when our kids were tiny, we were invited to a commune in Vancouver, B.C. Those people are still around: Stan Persky, George Bowering, a bunch of Canadians. George Stanley, perhaps. Warren Tallman was still alive. Robin Blaser lived across the bay, where he probably still lives. This group had what they call a commune and they invited my family and Jeremy [Prynne] to live with them for a couple of weeks during the summer. We thought it was larky enough to take them up on it. And one of the requirements was that everybody who was above a certain age had to make a meal one time. We got out a number of *The Georgia Straight*. Did you ever see that? You saw the totem pole we posed for? That's amazing. I didn't realize it was that widely distributed.

Sinclair: Those things never saw the light of day, but they came through the network.

Dorn: They saw the dark of night.

Sinclair: What hit me yesterday at the Arnolfini Gallery reading, Bristol, with Jeremy Prynne, seeing you there, was the missing presence who was the link for me, Charles Olson. Such a figure, presumably, for both of you?

Dorn: And in London for a while.

Sinclair: You mention in *Way West,* I think, Panna Grady's house in Regent's Park?

Dorn: Did you know Panna?

Sinclair: Yes, I did. I was around twenty. I went to make the film *Ah Sunflower!* with Allen Ginsberg in that house. She said: "Did you know Charles Olson was living here?" Which I didn't.

Dorn: He'd gone home by that time. He came over to see me. And lived for a time in Colchester. I was living in Victoria Road. He located the largest room and settled into it, which was his habit. People came to see him there. And Panna showed up in London and eventually she came up to see us and took him back. I can't remember what the circumstances were, but I do remember the taxi. It looked like an Arab taxi with everything piled on top and almost people hanging on. Imaginary people hanging on a bit like the Indian train that crashed the other day. Oh yes, those were amazing times.

Sinclair: Olson only traveled by taxi. He took a taxi to Dorchester.

Dorn: The shipping records were quite important in his work in Plymouth and Dorchester. He was really interested in tracing the contents of the passengers. And the goods.

Sinclair: Jeremy must, I guess, have been providing the bullets for you and for Olson.

Dorn: That's right. Jeremy came over from Cambridge to see him one evening, and Tom Clark came around. He was at Essex. Those were all notable evenings. He turned our house into a kind of salon. Those were beautiful active times. I mean not literary active, but more expanded. It was never merely literary with Charles. He liked the literary. But that was a pretty small role to him.

Sinclair: What I get from you, the sense of London at that time, the movement in the street and the passage of the eye across the landscape of the town, was easier and more open that it would be now?

Dorn: There was a lot more traffic and a lot less clutter. Absolutely. The traffic, as random as it sometimes seemed, seemed also purposeful. People actually did have things on their minds, no matter how strange those things were. They were actually going to a place no matter, if they arrived there, or if it was the wrong place. It was still part of the function and the structure, which was the point. There wasn't much business. People now are quite happy and proud to be busy. Nobody would have said they were busy then. Oh absolutely not that would have been an insult to oneself and one's auditor. Absolutely. There's an unconscious shift in what people now call attention, I think.

Emma Matthews (sound-recordist and editor): I wonder if it would be possible to go back to that attitude ever?

Dorn: Life is much more punishing now, in that sense. Punishment and abuse is so widespread. Once you break the unions and the possibilities of proletarian combination, all that's over with; you enslave people. Wage slavery was always a kind of a joke because it wasn't real slavery. But in fact it's not a joke and it is a real slavery. And it's not just blacks. It's everybody. It's not just pervasive, it's universal and it's ineradicable. If you rebel against it, that's considered some form of misbehavior.

For a poet the world is always static in the sense that you're a mass observer and you can't afford to care whether people are busy or not. You're a witness. I can comment on it, and I can disapprove of it, and I certainly have my taste, and I have my moral sense, but that's not actually my job.

Sinclair: Last night you and Jeremy both indicated that we've lived most of our lives in a war state. I remember you saying that you couldn't address the Vietnam War directly. But the question of addressing war seems to be nicely solved in what you're doing now the chemical war in your own body, the Clintonian shenanigans and Kosovo all meld.

Dorn: If everybody knows that there's a war, like with Vietnam, and everybody is morally compromised by it, then it's difficult to speak of that war. What do you say to someone: "Do you know there's a war going on?' Obviously not.

If people are in radical denial that there's war going on, then it is possible to direct your attention overtly and publicly and say: "No, you can't deny this because I'm not going to let you because it is war."

Sinclair: But even if they show us wars, they are virtual reality wars. Theoretically, they show us more than we ever saw and, at this same time, it's less of an experience.

Dorn: They wear you out with it, the tedium factor gets so heavy that you're willing to release that kind of attention to the care of others. In the audience last night there were undoubtedly people that had been convinced that the Albanians were a put-upon people, people for whom genocide and ethnic cleansing were strong signals and this gets received with no critical facility at all, none whatsoever. And you could tell that. It's all right to hate the Serbians because the Serbians are detestable and we've been told it's true. None of this is war in a sense. It's been settled, for sure.

Bomb an ancient capital into ruin. Don't apologize for it. On the contrary, brag about it. Take credit for it. Actually lie publicly that it was a mistake to bomb the Chinese Embassy as if that mattered. As if that could actually be defined as a mistake. It's just unbelievable. And then comes a moment when they say: "All right, that's it. Final take. The war's over. OK, it was a war after all." And when NATO is discussed, the Russians get insulted, and the World Health Organization really does have to look after that two tons of smallpox bacillus they have sitting in Moscow. We're paying their scientists not to go to work for anybody else, so we might as well do this or that. That wasn't awfully smart making them feel so neglected and insulted.

Sinclair: Is it knowable, what is happening to us, outside? Some kind of act of genocide?

Dorn: One man's genocide is another man's ethnic cleansing.

I think it's possible for two races of people to hate each other so thoroughly that they cannot do anything else with the situation.

If your foreign policy consists entirely of, "If you don't do what I say, I'm going to haul you off to the Hague and you'll be charged with war crimes, you're going to be incarcerated or hung," period, that is the whole of our foreign policy. That means you can declare anybody a bad person who happens to get in your way. You know the family from which Albright comes are a roving intervening band who think it can interfere on the grandest scale possible, the way no elected official could hope to do. They tell the Serbians: "You are not permitted to hate the people who have imposed the Muslim yoke on you for centuries. You don't get to remember the fields of Kosovo. It's not permitted you. Until you stop it, we're going to rain bombs on you." Well, if you're going to do that, that's a terrible punishment but it doesn't change anything. It's not going to make the Serbians love the Albanians. There's no apparent reason why the Serbs should love the Albanians.

The so-called media, which is a very obedient art form, has focused its attention where the Pentagon and the Department of State want and the toadying Foreign Office in the case of Britain. Britain is a lapdog. It doesn't even need to be stroked, it strokes itself in some strange way.

A book that Americans should be reading by Niall Ferguson, *The Pity of War.* Which so annoys the Germans because he's saying, "Well, actually, it should have been that Sir Edward Grey did not make war on the Germans and he was the only one who did because had the Kaiser been allowed to pull in the Luxembourg states and do what the Germans always do, we would be in exactly the same place that we are now without the damage. There'd be no gas." This book is just creating rancor. It's a good read for sure, deadly logic.

Sinclair: You said, "There are no parties, there's only function and drift." I like that. Is it still true?

Dorn: I think that with the recent miniwar within the war within the war within the war, named Kosovo and Belgrade, that's true. What is that thing you do when you punch in the base numbers? It's the base reference to all the other wars. It will go on and on and on. It's the base reference. Where the next war will be, of the Kosovo kind, we don't really know. It could be the sources of the Tigris and the Euphrates because the Kurds are a lot more numerous than anybody else who is in that situation. They're surrounded by enemies because they've got the Syrians and the Turks and the Iraqis. And, to one extent or another, the Iranians a little bit off that. We're talking about the prime conditions for creating an everlasting and powerful, intense and intensified enemy.

Sinclair: You're saying that we're folding back to Gilgamesh?

Dorn: (Laughs.) I think so. Good point, yeah. Ever since the Mongols arrived and sussed out the water supply of the Fertile Crescent, the first thing that anybody has done is bomb the sources. That's what Bush did when he started the war. The first thing he did was bomb the water supply. And he's just doing what Genghis Khan did. Except that he sent people in to actually spade it up.

Sinclair: This also destroys the sources of language. This is the first poetic.

Dorn: First, the water. Absolutely.

Sinclair: The other big subject you touched on last night was drugs.

Dorn: I'm anxious to incorporate the analysis of cancer drugs—from my own experience. Because they're obviously a huge industry. They're very expensive. When I pay $40 a day, the insurance company is paying $250. The Clintons' attempt, when they felt they could do something about all this, to attack big pharmaceuticals and bring the price down, was an instant and notable failure. They crashed immediately on that. They didn't do anything else after that actually. They were right. That was the heart of the problem. And it is because the statistics for cancer go up and up. We're not talking about breast cancer or some obviously inherited cancer; we're talking about environmentally induced cancers. The statistics are going up, and the drugs are being invented at pace, and the prices of all those drugs are increasing.

Sinclair: There is an element of Californian society, people like John Wayne, with a will towards cancer. There was an interview with a nightclub owner. He had gone out with Wayne, and he lit up a tipped cigarette and Wayne ripped it out of his mouth and said: "What kind of a fucking wimp are you? Take it straight, head on." Wayne picked up cancer making films in the desert.

Dorn: Remember John Wayne playing Genghis Khan. That was around Cedar City, Saint George, in the southeast corner of Utah where the drift comes. Above surface bombs. Before the underground tests. The plume came right around the mountain. Oh the cancer rates for there are off the clock. Yeah, it wasn't just John Wayne, you know. It was the whole crew. They were wallowing around in the dust as you do if you're making a film of Genghis Khan.

Sinclair: You give us such a sense of the West, the American West. Olson and so on. You're journeying now into the English West. Do you connect up with the mythology of the English West and what it means?

Dorn: Well, you know, it's all relative in that sense. You get on a train at Paddington and there's the thrill of heading west. And the country does have a broad base and it does open out and it does go all the way to Land's End. People who only buy shirts from the chain stores in America are amazed to learn that there's actually a place called Land's End. Yes. It's the West and things get a bit louder out here. You can feel it in the people. There's a certain kind of pride of being farther west than whatever east is. (Laughs.) And they've got the eclipse coming up— which is a big event. A big solar event.

Sinclair: About last night's reading in Bristol. The audience weren't expecting it and weren't aware, probably, of the significance of what was happening. Jeremy's reading was unforgiving.

Dorn: There's not much to hang on to except what you're able to manage. The rhetorical hangers and signals that go out from the ordinary writer such as my own aren't there. I guess Jeremy's the only one who's really insisted on it to that extent. Admirable, I think. It has to be true in the end. He nourished and laid constraints against my tendencies to blow things up, actually.

I think last night's reading was historically interesting and significant. But things of that nature have to be borne away by the witnesses. Sometimes I think that it's a shame that it's not captured. But, in a way, it's such a moment that capturing it is defeating it.

Bibliography

Selected Works by Ed Dorn

Poetry

The Newly Fallen. New York: Totem-Corinth, 1962.
Hands Up! New York: Totem-Corinth, 1963.
Geography. London: Fulcrum Press, 1965.
Idaho Out. London: Fulcrum Press, 1965.
North Atlantic Turbine. London: Fulcrum Press, 1967.
Gunslinger, Book I. Los Angeles: Black Sparrow Press, 1968.
Gunslinger, Book II. Los Angeles: Black Sparrow Press, 1969.
Twenty-Four Love Songs. West Newbury, Mass.: Frontier Press, 1969.
The Cycle. West Newbury, Mass.: Frontier Press, 1970.
Songs: Set Two, a Short Count. West Newbury, Mass.: Frontier Press, 1970.
Gunslinger, Book III: The Winterbook. West Newbury, Mass.: Frontier Press, 1971.
Recollections of Gran Apachería. Berkeley, Calif.: Turtle Island Foundation, 1974.
Collected Gunslinger (with Book IV). Berkeley, Calif.: Wingbow Press, 1974.
Collected Poems, 1956–1975. Bolinas, Calif.: Four Seasons Foundation, 1975.
Manchester Square (with Jennifer Dunbar). London: Permanent Press, 1975.
Hello La Jolla. Berkeley, Calif.: Wingbow Press, 1978.
Selected Poems. Bolinas, Calif.: Grey Fox Press, 1978.
Yellow Lola. Santa Barbara, Calif.: Cadmus Editions, 1981.
Captain Jack's Chaps—Houston/MLA. Madison, Wis.: Black Mesa Press, 1983.
Collected Poems, 1956–1983. 3rd. ed. San Francisco: Four Seasons, 1984.
From Abhorrences. Boise, Ida.: Limberlost Press, 1989.
Gunslinger. 2nd ed. Introduction by Marjorie Perloff.. Durham, N.C.: Duke University Press, 1989.
Abhorrences. Santa Rosa, Calif.: Black Sparrow Press, 1990.
The Denver Landing. Buffalo: Uprising Press, 1993.

High West Rendezvous. Buckfastleigh, South Devonshire, England: Etruscan Books, 1997.

Chemo Sábe. Boise, Ida.: Limberlost Press, 2001.

Way More West: New and Selected Poems. New York: Penguin, 2007.

Prose Fiction and Nonfiction

What I See in the Maximus Poems. Ventura, Calif.: Migrant Press, 1960.

A Bibliography on America for Ed Dorn. By Charles Olson. San Francisco: Four Seasons Foundation, 1964.

Rites of Passage. Buffalo: Frontier Press, 1965.

The Shoshoneans. New York: Wm. Morrow, 1966.

By The Sound. West Newbury, Mass.: Frontier Press, 1969.

Some Business Recently Transacted in the White World. West Newbury, Mass.: Frontier Press, 1971.

The Poet, The People, The Spirit. Vancouver: Talonbooks, 1976.

Roadtesting the Language: An Interview with Ed Dorn. By Stephen Fredman. San Diego: University of California, Archive for New Poetry, 1978.

Interviews. San Francisco: Four Seasons Press, 1980.

Views. San Francisco: Four Seasons Press, 1980.

By The Sound. New edition with preface by the author. Santa Rosa, Calif.: Black Sparrow Press, 1991.

Way West: Stories, Essays and Verse Accounts, 1963–1993. Santa Rosa, Calif.: Black Sparrow Press, 1993.

Translations (with Gordon Brotherston)

Our Word: Guerilla Poems from Latin America. London: Jonathan Cape/ Goliard, 1968.

Tree Between Two Walls. By José Emilio Pacheco. Los Angeles: Black Sparrow Press, 1971.

Caesar Vallejo. London: Penguin, 1975.

Image of the New World. Translated from Yucatecan and Nahuatl. London: Thames & Hudson, 1979.

The Sun Unwound: Original Texts from Occupied America. Berkeley, Calif.: North Atlantic Press, 1999.

Recordings

The North Atlantic Turbine. Fulcrum Press Records, London, 1967.

Gunslinger Books I, II & The Cycle. S Press Tapes, Munich, 1970.

Satiric Verses. Alternative Radio, Boulder, Colorado, 2001.

Critical Studies on Ed Dorn

Beach, Christopher. "Migrating Voices in the Poetry of Edward Dorn." In *ABC of Influence: Ezra Pound and the Remaking of American Poetic Tradition.* Berkeley and Los Angeles: University of California Press, 1992.

Clark, Tom. *A World of Difference: Edward Dorn.* Berkeley, Calif.: North Atlantic Press, 2002.

"Edward Dorn, American Heretic." Special issue, *Chicago Review* 49, nos. 3–4 and 50, no. 1 (2004).

Elmborg, James K. *"A Pageant of Its Time": Edward Dorn's Slinger and the Sixties.* Studies in Modern Poetry 6. New York: Peter Lang, 1998.

Fox, Willard. *Robert Creeley, Edward Dorn, and Robert Duncan: A Reference Guide.* Boston: G. K. Hall, 1989.

McPheron, William. *Edward Dorn.* Boise, Ida.: Boise State University, 1989.

Paul, Sherman. *The Lost America of Love: Rereading Robert Creeley, Edward Dorn, and Robert Duncan.* Baton Rouge: Louisiana State University Press, 1981.

Sagetrieb 15, no. 3, 1996. Special issue on Dorn.

Streeter, David. *A Bibliography of Ed Dorn.* New York: Phoenix Bookshop, 1974.

Wesling, Donald, ed. *Internal Resistances: The Poetry of Ed Dorn.* Berkeley and Los Angeles: University of California Press, 1985.